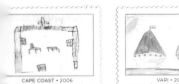
CAPE COAST • 2006

VARI • 2007

SAINT GEORGE'S • 2007

XEGÜINACABAJ • 2008

BISSAU • 2005

CONAKRY • 2005

BARTICA • 2005

P9-DVS-118
PORT-AU-PRINCE • 2007

CHOLUTECA • 2008

BUDAPEST • 2007

REYKJAVIK • 2008

PHAGI • 2006

JAKARTA • 2006

TEHRAN • 2009

DOHUK • 2007

DUBLIN • 2007

HERZILIAH • 2006

MILANO • 2006

KINGSTON • 2007

TSUSHIMA • 2006

AMMAN • 2006

ALMATY • 2008

KAKAMEGA • 2008

EITA • 2006

SEOUL • 2006

PYONGYANG • 2008

KUWAIT CITY • 2009

TOGUZ-BULAK • 2008

VIENTIANE • 2006

RIGA • 2007

BEYROUTH • 2006

THABA BOSIU • 2008

MONROVIA • 2005

TRIPOLI • 2008

VADUZ • 2008

VILNIUS • 2007

LUXEMBOURG • 2009

SKOPJE • 2007

AMONDRA • 2008

LILONGWE • 2007

AMPANG • 2006

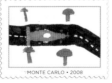
MALE • 2009

NGOA • 2006

MGARR • 2008

DELAP • 2006

NOUAKCHOTT • 2008

TROU AUX BICHES • 2008

SAN MIGUEL • 2008

POHNPEI • 2006

CHISINAU • 2007

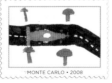
MONTE CARLO • 2008

BAGANUUR • 2008

PODGORICA • 2007

BOULAD SGUIR • 2008

ILHA DE MOÇAMBIQUE • 2007

MANDALAY • 2006

WINDHOEK • 2008

NAURU • 2006

KATHMANDU • 2006

HELMOND • 2007

AUCKLAND • 2006

ESTELÍ • 2008

NIAMEY • 2006

JOS • 2006

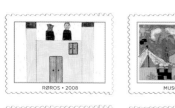 RØROS • 2008
 MUSCAT • 2008
 SHEIKHUPURA • 2006
 KOROR • 2006
 PANAMA CITY • 2008
 PORT MORESBY • 2006
 ASUNCIÓN • 2006
 LIMA • 2007

 QUEZON CITY • 2006
 KRAKOW • 2007
 LISBOA • 2005
 DOHA • 2009
 CRAIOVA • 2007
 SAINT PETERSBURG • 2006
 KIGALI • 2008
 MANSION • 2007

 CASTRIES • 2007
 CALLIQUA • 2007
 APIA • 2006
 SAN MARINO • 2008
 SÃO TOMÉ • 2007
 RIYAD • 2009
 DAKAR • 2005
NOVI SAD • 2007

 BAIE LAZARE • 2008
 MAKENI • 2005
 SINGAPORE • 2006
 BRATISLAVA • 2007
 LJUBLJANA • 2007
 HONIARA • 2006
 HARGEISSA • 2008
SOWETO • 2008

 ZARAGOZA • 2005
 BATTARAMULLA • 2009
 KHARTOUM • 2008
 BROKOPONDO • 2007
 MBABANE • 2007
 KÄVLINGE • 2007
 UZWIL • 2008
 DAMASCUS • 2006

 KHOJAND • 2008
 MWANZA • 2008
 CHUMPHON • 2006
 DILI • 2006
 LOME • 2006
 NUKU'ALOFA • 2006
 PORT OF SPAIN • 2007
 TUNIS • 2008

 ISTANBUL • 2007
 ASHGABAT • 2008
 FUNAFUTI • 2006
 KAMPALA • 2008
 KIEV • 2007
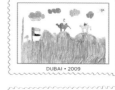 DUBAI • 2009
 ELTHAM • 2007
 LOS ANGELES • 2006

 URUGUAY • 2006
 FERGANA • 2008
 PORT VILA • 2006
 MARACAIBO • 2007
 BEN TRE • 2006
 SANHAM • 2008
 LUSAKA • 2007
 HARARE • 2008

Children of the World

Children of the World

How We Live, Learn, and Play in Poems, Drawings, and Photographs

Anthony Asael

and

Stéphanie Rabemiafara

UNIVERSE

Published by Universe Publishing
A Division of Rizzoli International Publications, Inc.
300 Park Avenue South
New York, NY 10010
www.rizzoliusa.com

Project Editor: Candice Fehrman
Book Design: Susi Oberhelman

All the statistics listed in the back of this book are extracted from UNICEF's State of
the World's Children reports published in 2007 and 2009.

Children all over the world speak many languages, eat many foods, and play many
sports. In the fun facts for this book, we have only listed the official or most common
languages, the most popular foods, and the most popular sports or activities.

2011 2012 2013 2014 / 10 9 8 7 6 5 4 3 2 1

Printed in China

ISBN-13: 978-0-7893-2267-8

Library of Congress Catalog Control Number: 2011921538

Art in All of Us

Art in All of Us (AiA) is a global not-for-profit organization dedicated to stimulating the creativity and curiosity for other cultures within children using art. Founded by photographers Anthony Asael and Stéphanie Rabemiafara in 2005, AiA has inspired more than 26,000 children from 350 schools, in all 192 United Nations member countries.

Through photography, drawings, and poetry, children—and adults—are able to learn about and understand cultural similarities and differences. Since 2005, AiA has been developing a variety of programs, which are currently being implemented in schools and communities around the globe to help encourage their mandate of cross-cultural understanding and to empower a sense of global citizenship.

By partnering with UNICEF and working with local NGOs and volunteers, AiA has allowed children in every country to learn about the lives of other children from every corner of the earth. By creating awareness we are building tolerance, opening eyes and minds, and encouraging a peaceful and tolerant future.

On every page of this book, the lives of children around the world are being represented: their realities, their dreams, their ambitions, and their voices are being expressed, most for the first time, on a global scale. From these pages, we hope to empower a global understanding between cultures, generations, and individuals, which we hope will lead to building a greater tolerance and cross-cultural understanding, among children and adults. We believe in the power of art to transform lives, which, in turn, can transform our world.

For more information, visit www.artinallofus.org.

Contents

Foreword

© UNICEF

Supported by UNICEF

This extraordinary book is an adventure into the creative minds of children. It is the brainchild of two talented photographers, Anthony Asael and Stéphanie Rabemiafara, who presented the idea of offering children in all 192 United Nations member countries the chance to express themselves through art.

UNICEF is a proud supporter of the project, called Art in All of Us, which also has the global backing of hundreds of volunteers, organizations, and corporations. In four years and 620,000 kilometers, Asael and Rabemiafara visited 310 primary schools and helped spur the creation of 25,000 artworks all done by children—of different cultures, religions, and geographical backgrounds. This book displays some of these along with a snapshot of the 160,000 photographs provided by Asael and Rabemiafara.

The result is a colorful ensemble of creative pieces from around the world—from Belgium to Benin—that reflect the uniqueness of each background, yet also the similarities that run through childhood. As one student in Syria noted after looking at some of the other artwork, "there is no difference between us and the children from other countries."

Art in All of Us has provided thousands of children the opportunity to express themselves using the universal language of art. This book showcases photography and art as a vehicle to promote respect, tolerance, and peace and build a better world for children and their families.

Ann M. Veneman
Executive Director, UNICEF
2005–2010

How This Book Works

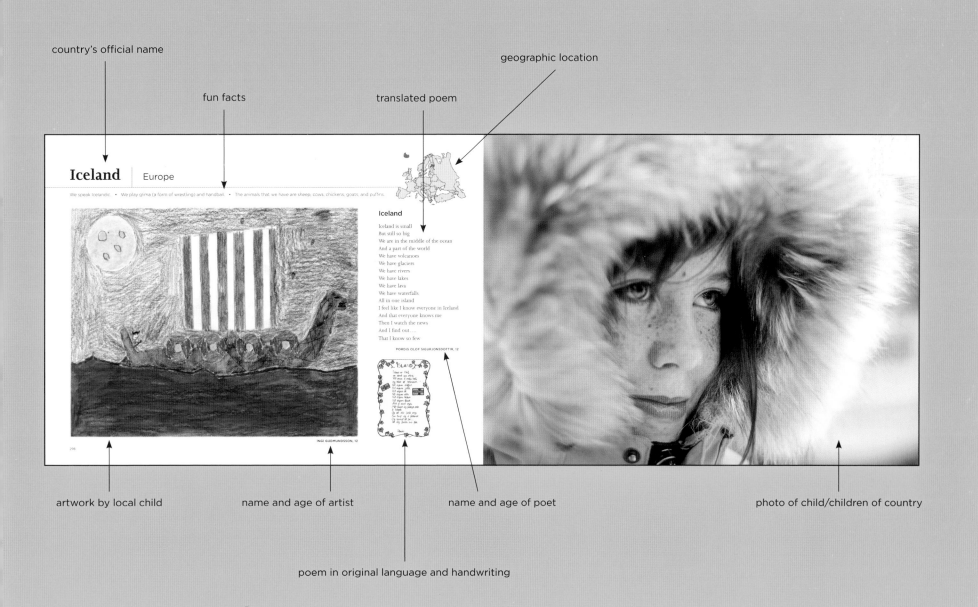

country's official name

fun facts

translated poem

geographic location

Iceland | Europe

We speak Icelandic. • We play glima (a form of wrestling) and handball. • The animals that we have are sheep, cows, chickens, goats, and puffins.

Iceland

Iceland is small
But still so big
We are in the middle of the ocean
And a part of the world
We have volcanoes
We have glaciers
We have rivers
We have lakes
We have lava
We have waterfalls
All in one island
I feel like I know everyone in Iceland
And that everyone knows me
Then I watch the news
And I find out....
That I know so few

PORDIS OLOF SIGURJONSDOTTIR, 12

INGI GUDMUNDSSON, 12

artwork by local child

name and age of artist

name and age of poet

photo of child/children of country

poem in original language and handwriting

Introduction

I met photographers Anthony Asael and Stéphanie Rabemiafara six years ago in Chile. When they told me about their project, its objectives, and the material that they wanted to compile, I thought it was a fantastic initiative that should be carried out. The idea of being able to create art with children from each of the 192 United Nations member countries immediately appealed to me because it is completely in line with my convictions. Every day I am more certain that art is one of the best ways—or excuses—to bring people all over the world closer together and break down barriers of prejudice, geographic distance, or culture.

In their travels, the photographers met more than 18,000 children, took close to 160,000 photographs, and collected close to 25,000 works of art. They used a similar methodology in each workshop, which included a presentation about the project, followed by a session about composing and creating photographs. Then they held a dynamic brainstorming session so that the children could internalize and understand the notions of culture and cultural identity. They had drawing and writing workshops, and interactive geography games, using photos taken in other countries of children just like them. Art in All of Us (AiA) chose to target children from eight to twelve years old, the ages at which Anthony and Stéphanie found that innocence and creativity are still expressed in a free and spontaneous way.

In order for AiA to be a success, a huge amount of organization and logistical planning had to be put in place. Anthony and Stéphanie had to consider the coordination of thousands of practical details, and all at a very low cost. They scheduled each workshop from a distance, three to eight months in advance. They organized itineraries, contacted translators, got vaccines, secured transportation and food, raised funds, and successfully sent hundreds of drawings and poems from one corner of the earth to another. This project could not have been completed without the help of UNICEF, which supported the photographers in more than ninety countries. UNICEF staff helped AiA coordinate workshops, arrange visas, obtain authorization from ministries of education, find out about security and precautionary measures in order to travel through areas of unrest, and much more.

Pursuing such a lofty dream, as Anthony and Stéphanie learned, comes with its own set of unique complications and dangers. It took two and a half years to get permission to enter North Korea, for example, but they persisted until they were able to meet with a school of children and work with them. (AiA was the first foreign art project in this closed country.) They traveled through regions devastated by earthquakes, floods, wars, rebellions, attacks, and military coups. They traveled in different types of violent and threatening environments, and escaped shipwrecks and muggings by a matter of minutes. Anthony even spent a short amount of time in a Jordanian jail, but not by any fault of his own.

During one of their last trips to Chile, Anthony and Stéphanie told me a story that well represents the mixture of adventure, magic, and luck which enveloped the long trip and made this book possible. They wanted to visit Nauru, a small Pacific island with only 10,000 inhabitants, which does not have its own port or airline, potable water, electricity twenty-four hours a day, or a regular supply of fuel. When checking in for the trip, they were informed that the return flight was canceled for an indefinite period of time. They had three options: to not travel, to go without knowing when they would be able to come back, or to go and return on the same airplane, on the next morning's flight. They took the third option at the risk of not being able to have the workshop, or—even worse—missing the flight and not knowing when or how they would be able to return.

They landed on the island at 4:00 p.m., but all the schools had finished for the day at 1:30 p.m. They only knew the name of the school and that the teacher's name was Joanie. Like all foreigners who arrive in Nauru, Anthony and Stéphanie had to leave their passports with the head of immigration. According to local law, they could not get their passports back until two days later, but given that they planned to leave the next morning, they negotiated to get the passports directly from the Minister of the Interior.

They did not find taxis when they left the airport. Since there is no fuel on the island, the only cars are those belonging to the twelve official ministers. They started asking pedestrians if they knew the teacher, and they were successful on the third try.

The passerby turned out to be the teacher's uncle and also worked in the Ministry of Education. They reached the teacher and told her about the schedule and their rapid departure, in less than fourteen hours. It was already 6:30 p.m. and, as if it were the most natural thing in the world, the teacher suggested that they gather the students together and have the workshop that very night. They covered the entire island in the minister's truck, picking up all the children, whose parents gave them permission without any problems.

Since they had arrived at the school very late, they had to ask the Minister of Energy to provide electric lights for the three or four hours of workshops. The activities with the children were a success and the workshops took place in a room full of smiles, joy, energy, and curiosity. The children, the teacher, and Anthony and Stéphanie left the school at 1:00 a.m. They went more than twenty hours without sleep and had eaten very little. When they dropped off the last child at his house at 2:00 a.m., in the complete darkness of the streets, they remembered that they had to recover their passports from the Minister of the Interior. The minister came to the door in pajamas, with sleepy eyes, and gave them their stamped passports. There were three hours left for them to sleep before catching the return flight, and they had fulfilled their mission.

The book that you have in your hands contains some of the magic of Nauru, and the beauty created when children are given the chance to express themselves. It is a book made by the dreams and realities of children, but it is also a product of Anthony and Stéphanie's tireless dedication and ceaseless ambition. They put every effort into each detail, from the first to the last workshop, and from the initial concept of the book to the final result, and returned from their long tour around the world with an invaluable treasure trove of photos, drawings, and poems created by the children of the world.

Roberto Edwards

Roberto Edwards
Director, Fundación América

Afghanistan | Asia

We speak Pashtun and Dari. • We eat rice and meat dishes and drink *chai* (tea). • We play soccer, cricket, and *buzkashi* (a game like polo).

Our Country

I love this country and its grounds
I love its desert, its forests, I love this country
I love the people of this country,
I love the rivers
I love the farmers
I love the shepherds.

NAZILA GRAN, 10

FATAH MOHAMMAD, 12

Albania | Europe

We speak Albanian. • We eat *tave kosi* (meat baked in yogurt) and *fasule* (boiled dried beans). • We play basketball and soccer.

ARMANDO BEKTASHI, 14

I Am the Lord of My Destiny

Life is beautiful
But sometimes not
Good or bad,
I'm the lord of my fate

If I want to change
It depends on me
And if I change
It will change my destiny

And myself too
There are a lot of things that I want to reach,
And perhaps I can't
But I have to think,
To do something
Because I am the Lord of my destiny

ARLINDA SELA, 14

Jam zot i fatit tim

Jeta është e bukur
Por edhe e shpifur
E mirë por edhe e keqe
Jam zot i fatit tim

Nëse dua të ndryshoj
varet nga unë
dhe nëse ndryshoj
edhe jeta e fatit do të ndyshoje

Ka shumë gjëra në jetë
që ndoshta s'i arrij
por duhet të mendoj të bëj diçka
sepse jam zot i fatit tim

| Algeria | Africa |

We speak Arabic and Berber. • We eat *couscous* with lamb and *tajine* (meat and vegetable stew). • We play soccer, basketball, and volleyball.

HAOUA HARDI, 11

Algeria

Algeria is beautiful
The countryside is vast
Its full moon is beautiful
Its honey flavor fruits
The Casbah* is white

She attracts the sun
Beautiful like the sky
Like the sunset
Are the oldest cures
Just like the doves

MELIHA MEHDI, 11

* Algiers's citadel and traditional quarter

L'Algérie

L'Algérie est belle ✶ elle attir le soleil sur
elle
La nature est grande ✶ belle comme le ciel

La pleine lune est belle ✶ comme le coucher du
soleil

Les fruits aux goût de miel ✶ guérissent les
plus vieilles

La casba est blanche ✶ comme les
colombes.

Andorra | Europe

We speak Catalan, French, and Spanish. • We eat wild boar, *paella* (a rice dish), and ham with honey. • We play outside—skiing, canoeing, and hiking.

Andorra is a small country,
It may be small, but people have really big hearts.
Tourism fills the mountains where rare animals live.
Small, big, it doesn't matter, they live happily.

The mountains sometimes parade
Covered in snow
We never know when, it changes a lot!
The sky is blue, with that we don't need a big ocean!

MATTHEW ROBINSON, 9

CARLA AND ANDREA, 10

Andorre est un petit pays
Petit certa mais le cœur des gens est bien grand.
Le tourisme remplit les montagnes où vivent des espèces animales rares.
Petit, grand peu importe ils vivent heureux

Les hautes montagne qui défilent
couvertent de neige parfois.
On ne sait jamais quand ça change souvent.
Le ciel est bleu avec ça on a pas besoin du vaste océan.

Angola | Africa

We speak Portuguese.   •   We eat *calulú* (a fish and vegetable dish) and tropical fruits like mangoes and papayas.   •   We play soccer, basketball, and handball.

Festa de Carnaval Numa casa

VALIDNA MANUEL, 9

My Country

My country is big and beautiful.
It's part of the African continent
Jungle's path
People's path
Tired people!!!
Path of the bush
Path of the flowers
Flowers of love!!!
My country has houses, schools, animals, playgrounds.
I like my country
We, the children of Angola, are very happy.
We are happy because my country is beautiful and pretty.

DINAMENE CALETE, 9

O meu país

O meu país é grande e belo.
Faz parte do continente africano.

Caminho do mato
Caminho da gente
gente cansada!!!

Caminho do mato
Caminho das flores
flores de amor!!!

O meu país tem casas, Escolas, animais, parques Xantes.
Eu gosto do meu país nós crianças de Angola, estamos muito fez.

Gostamos feliz porque o meu país é belo e bonito.

Antigua & Barbuda | Central America

We speak English. • We eat tropical fruits, meat with rice, and *fungee* (spoon bread with cornmeal and okra). • We play cricket, soccer, and basketball.

Antigua nice sweet like paradise
Antigua is nice … shout it for the world
to see
If you love Antigua, participate
Come celebrate
This is my island in the sun
Jamming from since time begun
Check out the places to go and
Wash out your faces,
In one of our 365 beaches

JOSEPH KWAMAYNE, 10

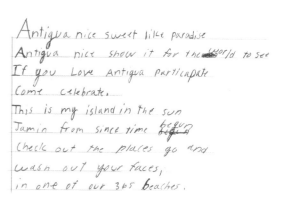

KEIANN AND ASHMANIE, 11

Argentina | South America

We speak Spanish.   •   We eat many beef dishes, such as *empanadas* (meat turnovers).   •   We play soccer and *el pato* (a game played on horseback).

My flag is a star
Enlightening my path,
My flag is a sun
Enlightening my path,
My flag is a moon
Cheering up my path,
My flag is a big flag
A flag I will never forget.

Its blue is like the sea,
Its white is like the snow on the mountains,
Its yellow shines like gold,
And its splendor
Is like the flag, the Argentinean flag.

ANDREA LILIANA ROJO, 9

MILENA CASCO AND LUCAS DEGREGORIO, 9

Mi bandera es una estrella
que ilumina mi camino,
mi Bandera es un sol
que arrumbra mi camino,
mi Bandera es una luna
que alegra mi camino,
mi Bandera es una gran Bandera,
la Bandera a la que nunca olvidaré.

Su azul es como el mar
su blanco es como la nieve de las montañas,
su amarillo brillante es como el oro,
y su gran esplendor
es como la bandera, la bandera Argentina

Armenia | Asia

We speak Armenian and Russian. • We eat *dolma* (stuffed grape or cabbage leaves) and lots of fruit. • We play soccer, tennis, and basketball.

EMMA GARDILIAN, 11

My beautiful Armenia,
The flower of my heart,
The light and fire of my eyes,
Pear, grape, pomegranate, and apricot.

My dear Armenia,
A whole sea of letters,
A library of manuscripts,
My beautiful, my marvelous Armenia.

LIANA HARUTUNYAN, 11

Australia | Oceania

We speak English and Aboriginal languages. • We eat steak, meat pies, seafood, and french fries. • We play cricket, Australian football, and rugby.

JAALA, 12

Australia is a country,
New but so alive
A fuzzy feeling you get inside
From meeting a friend's eyes

The outback sun is ferocious
But kind at some times too
Growing plants and flora
For so many people to view

A mateship is a thing we Aussies have
A feeling that lets you soar
An indescribable state of mind
That has you coming back for more

The footy, a sport, a reunion,
For races both white and black
Multiculturalism, don't you adore it?
All different races, none we do not have

So next time you see an Australian,
Remember the things I've said
We always live life to the fullest,
Right until we're dead

FLETCHER HORNE, 12

Austria | Europe

We speak German and other regional dialects. • We eat *Wiener Schnitzel* (baked veal), goulash, and sausages. • We play winter sports and soccer.

Life in Austria

The sun shines
The Danube rustles
Children are happy
Cows graze

Life in the countryside

The sun shines
Cows graze
Goats bleat
Horses snicker

CAROLIN, 8

LAURA FRANZ, 9

Leben in Österreich
Die Sonne scheint.
Die Donau rauscht.
Die Kinder sind glücklich.
Die Kühe grasen.

Leben am Land
Die Sonne scheint.
Die Kühe grasen.
Die Ziegen meckern.
Die Pferde wiehern.

Azerbaijan | Asia

We speak Azeri and Russian. • We eat *plov* (rice dish), meat kababs, and *piti* (lamb broth with potatoes and peas). • We play soccer and like wrestling.

MAMISOVA, 12

Vətən.

Vətən ana kimidir,
Ana da vətən kimi.
Hər ikisi əzizdir
Azərbaycan xalqına.

Müharibə olmasa,
Sevinər hər bir uşaq,
Müharibə olmasa,
Sevinər hər bir insan

Qoy Azərbaycan xalqı var olsun,
Sevinc ana yar olsun.
Daim ulu tanrımız,
Xalqımızı qorusun.

Motherland

Our motherland is like a mother to us
Our mother is like motherland to us
Both are venerable
For the love of Azerbaijan

When there are no battles
The people is happy
When there are no battles
Everyone is delighted

May Azerbaijan be healthy
May our mother be blessed,
God Almighty
Protect our love.

BAGIROVA NILUFAR, 10

Bahamas | Central America

We speak English. • We eat *conch* (large mollusk), *chicken souse* (spicy chicken soup), and potato bread. • We play soccer and we like boat racing.

KESHONE MORLEY, 9

The Bahamas is a pretty place,
It looks better than space!
The stars are so bright
You better don't lose your sight!

It has beautiful beaches
And so are our peaches!
Did I forget the crab fest?
Oh, it is the best!

The sun is so hot,
You will get a tan spot,
The sky is so beautiful,
It will make your day restful.

So when you think about paradise
The Bahamas is the place!

JADA SWEETING, 9

Bahrain | Asia (Middle East)

We speak Arabic, English, and Hindi. • We eat *beryani* (spicy rice and meat dish), and *rottab* (fresh dates). • We play soccer, basketball, and volleyball.

FATIMA JASSIN RIDHA, 10

Bahrain, you're my treasure
Bahrain, you build my future
People come here to learn
People come here to earn

A small kingdom that promotes freedom
A land full of sand
A land that helps the birds fly
A land that guides the blind.

You're the country of luck
Our great ancestors found,
Your foundation is sure
Our tomorrow's secure.

ANFAL HUSSAIN, 12

Bangladesh | Asia

We speak Bangla. • We eat various rice dishes, fried vegetables, fish, and *dal* (spicy lentil-based soup). • We play soccer, field hockey, and cricket.

FATIMA KHATUN TAMIN, 10

Oh! My Golden Bangladesh

Golden Bangladesh,
How green the country is!
Golden Bangladesh,
The wind blows throughout the country,
We get up in the morning,
Hearing the nice birds singing,
This is my Golden Bangladesh

ROCKY BUL, 10

আমার সোনার দেশ,

সোনার বাংলা দেশ।

সবুজ শ্যামলে ঘেরা এই দেশ,

সোনার বাংলা দেশ,

আমাদের দেশের বাতাস আসে,

সকালে স্বাধীন আকে ছুটে বোঝে,

আমাদের কোকের নাম বাংলা দেশ,

সোনার বাংলা দেশ,

Barbados | Central America

We speak English. • We eat seafood, *pepperpot* (a spicy stew), and rice dishes. • We play cricket and soccer, and we like surfing and scuba diving.

AARON HEWITT, 11

Barbados

Beautiful Barbados
Near the Caribbean Sea
How I love this little island
It means so much to me
Calypso is my favorite song
Sometimes it is very long
Makes you want to jump and wave
Makes you want to move your waist.

KENDRA BOVELL, 11

Barbados
Beautiful Barbados,
Near the Caribbean Sea
How I love this little island
It means so much to me
Calypso is our favourite song
Sometimes it is very long
Makes you want to jump and wave
Makes you want to move your waist

Belarus | Europe

We speak Belarusian and Russian. • We eat rye bread, *uha* (fish soup), and *draniki* (potato pancakes). • We play soccer and ice hockey.

Belarus

I love my dear Belarus,
The boundless ribbons of the roads.
Lead to towns and villages,
Just cross the threshold.
And you will find:
A blue sky, rye fields
And meadows' silk grass.
Birds' songs and sun's smile,
You wouldn't find better paths!

M. TREMVEKOVA, 11

Беларусь

Люблю Беларусь маю родную,
Бяскрайнія стужкі дарог.
Вядуць яны ў горад і вёску,
Ты тольки ступі за парог.
Блакітнае неба, жытнёвае паля
І луга шаўковы мурог.
Птушыныя песні і сонца ўсмешка,
Ты лепшых не знойдзеш дарог

LIZA LINCHENKO, 10

44

Belgium | Europe

We speak French, Dutch, and German. • We eat fish, mussels, waffles, and french fries with mayonnaise. • We play soccer and *boules* (lawn bowling).

MARJAN SUFFYS, KELSEY DEPUYDT, 12

Expedition in Belgium

Belgium may be very small
But we do appreciate parties!

The women go shopping
And the men drink beer!

Chips are also very special
In Belgium we eat them all the time!

The Belgians gladly travel
And study well at school!

HAYLEY ROLLEZ, 12

Belize | Central America

We speak Spanish, English, and Creole. • We eat *panades* (corn shells with beans) and *escabeche* (onion soup). • We play soccer and basketball.

HENRY FIGUEROA, 8

My Country Belize

In my country Belize
There are beautiful mountains
There are animals,
Like our national animal called Tapir
Or our national bird: Toucan
There are also beautiful islands
As well as wonderful ruins
That are called: Caracol*, Xunantunich**, Pac-bitun***
And there are also other birds
Flying from branch to branch

ERIC RUANO, 11

* Large Maya archaeological site
** Maya archaeological site
*** Ceremonial Maya ballroom

mº pais Belice

En mº pais Belice hay montaña
muy bella hay animales como el
animal national se llama Tapir.
y el pajaro national Toucan. y
Tanbien hay islas muy bellas
de Belice y tambien hay
ruinas muy bellas se llama
caracol, xunantonich, packbitun
y tonbien hay pajaros bolando
de rama en rama.

Benin | Africa

We speak French and other regional dialects. • We eat yams, sweet potatoes, beans and rice, and fried bananas. • We play soccer and lawn bowling.

Benin my dear country,
Country of quiet democracy
Country of peacefulness and brotherhood
Country of solidarity and conviviality.

Benin my dear country,
Pacific country
Terrific country.
Dynamic country and full of determination
Country of decentralization and cooperation
Country of modernization and democratization.
Happy country
Peaceful country
Long live Benin,
Long live Africa   **NOUATIN SABINE, 10**

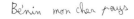

Bénin mon cher pays
Pays de démocratie apaisée
Pays de tranquillité et de fraternité
Pays de solidarité et de convivialité
Bénin mon cher pays
Pays pacifique
Pays magnifique
Pays dynamique et de détermination
Pays de décentralisation et de coopération
Pays de modernisation et de démocratisation
Pays toujours gais
Pays toujours en Paix
vive le Bénin
vive l'Afrique

GBENOUVONON FLORENT, 11

Bhutan | Asia

We speak Dzongkha. • We eat rice, hot curries, *thukpa* (noodle soup), and *momo* (Tibetan ravioli). • We play soccer, but our national sport is archery.

YESHI DEMA, 10

Bhutan is a land of greenery,
I wish I could describe its scenery,
The birds are chirping so merrily,
And we always listen to them so happily,
When it rains it's too gloomy,
But when we look on the bright side the flowers are blooming!
We feel like the mountains are so high,
When we stand on the top we feel like touching the sky!
Bhutan is in the Himalayan range,
But it always feels kind of strange!
This school that I study in is very fun,
But when I go out it doesn't feel fun without the sun
People tell stories about monsters
That they have really encountered!

SAUHARAN THATIPAMULA NENKATA, 9

Bolivia | South America

We speak many languages, but mostly Spanish, Quechua, and Aymara. • We eat rice dishes and quinoa soups. • We play soccer and like wrestling.

My Bolivia

I. On the shores of Lake Titicaca*,
The sun shines beautifully,
Boats keep passing by,
Fishes swim deep in the lake.

II. And the people arrive in Copacabana**
In the presence of the Copacabana's Virgin
To be blessed
With lots of faith and devotion.

III. And in the city of Oruro
They go with the Virgin of Socaben
To pray and give grace,
For being a good Virgin.

IV. And in yungas*** they go to pick up
Fruits, tangerines, pineapples,
And other fruits, like
Grapes and oranges,
Watermelon and bananas.

GERMAN PORTUGAL CUEVAS, 13

* One of the highest commercially navigable lakes in
the world, on the border of Bolivia and Peru
** City on the shores of Lake Titicaca
*** Warm valleys found on both sides of the Andes
around Peru or Bolivia

Mi Bolivia

I
En las orillas del lago titicaca;
brilla el hermoso sol,
y los barcos pasan a cada rato,
y los peces nadan a lo profundo del lago.

II
y las personas llegan a ropacabana,
aode la virgen de ropacabana
a hacerse bendecir
con mucha Fe y mucha devoción

III
Y en la ciudad de oruro
bandonde la Virgen del socabon
a rezar y dar gracias,
Por ser buena virgen

IV
Y en yungas ban a recojor,
Frutas, mandarinas, piñas
y otras Frutas como,
La uva y la naranja,
La zandia y los platanos.

LISET MAMANI ROMERO, 11

54

Bosnia & Herzegovina | Europe

We speak Serbo-Croatian. • We eat a lot of pies: *burek* (meat pie), *sirnica* (cheese pie), and cabbage pie. • We play basketball, tennis, and soccer.

ANEL GRADASCENIC, 12

Bosnia my homeland,
My pride, my peace
My family and my sister
It's small but it's strong
Full of happiness, wishes and hope
It may not have achieved much
But it didn't give up
It's still on it's feet
And it's coming to its goal:
Becoming better!
The rivers are clear,
The sky is blue,
I like it just the way it is
Bosnia, my pride, my home.

ADNA ARSLANOVIC, 10

Bosna, moja domovina
moj pomos
moj mir
moja porodica i moj spas
mala je al snazna
puna nadosti i želja
i puna made i veselja
možda nije mnogo postigla
al se nije predala
još uvjek je na nogama
i sve se više bliži cilju
sve je više napredniya
rjeke su bistne
nebo je vedro
ja je volim onakvu kakva jeste
Bosna, moj pomos, moja domovim

Botswana | Africa

We speak Setswana, but our official language is English. • We eat *bogobe* (porridge) at most meals. • We play soccer and like track-and-field events.

Botswana

Botswana Botswana
A beautiful country
A country of Africa
A country of black people

Botswana Botswana
What a beautiful country
A country full of peace
Understanding people and team work
A country of the Botswana people
People with a good heart,
Loving and respectful people

Botswana Botswana
What a beautiful country
Botswana the land covered with green grass
A land with trees with ripe fruits
Botswana a country of beautiful animals
A country of tourism
Botswana Botswana
A country of happiness.

CHIPO HAMALUBA, 8

PATIENCE PILANE, 12

Botswana

Botswana Botswana
lepatshe le lentle,
lepatshe la Aarica,
lepatshe la batho ba
ba itsho.

Botswana Botswana
A lepatshe le lentle,
lepatshe le le tleleeng
Kagiso, Kutlwano le
tirisanyo mmogo, Lepatshe
la Batswana, batho ba
ba pelo ntle, ba ba lorato,
ba ba maitseo.

Botswana Botswana
A lepatshe le lentle
Botswana lepatshe
le le apesitweng kabo
e tala, lepatshe la
ditlhare tse di ungwileng
Lepatshe la diphologolo
tse dintle Botswana,
Botswana lepatshe la
baitumelo

Brazil | South America

We speak many languages, but mostly Portuguese. • We eat *feijoada* (black beans with meat) and rice. • We play soccer and beach volleyball.

Brazil

The flag of Brazil has several colors:
Green, yellow, blue, and white
Green like leaves
Yellow like the sun
Blue like the sea
White like the clouds

Brazil:
With a B, I write Beijo (kiss)
With an R, I write Rio (river)
With an A, I write Amor (love)
With an S, I write Samba
With an I, I write Ilha (island)
With an L, I write Lindeza (lovely)

And with these small letters I write
Brazil from the bottom of my heart.

BIANCA DA SILVA AROYO ZARATY, 10

ANA DIAS GOES, 10

Brazil
A bandeira do Brasil tem
as cores verde, amarelo, azul e branca
verde como as folhas
Amarelo como o sol
Azul como o mar e
branco como as nuvens.

Brazil
com B escrevo Beijo
com R escrevo Rio
com A escrevo Amor
com S escrevo Samba
com I escrevo Ilha
com L escrevo Lindeza

em essas 6 letrinhas
escrevo Brasil no fundo do meu coração

Brunei | Asia

We speak Malay and English.   •   We eat a variety of spicy rice dishes, *pais lauk* (grilled fish), and *soto* (noodle soup).   •   We play soccer.

Kampung Ayer

KHAIRIAH HAFIZAH BINTI AND ABDEL AZIZ, 10

Negera Brunei Darussalam

I live in Brunei.
I like my country.
During the holiday, I play soccer.
My country has a flag.
I am Muslim boy.
I live in Berakas*.
The color of my country is yellow, red, black, and white.
I like blue.
I like to eat chicken and rice and to drink melon juice.
I always go to the beach.
My school is the Bakti Dewa School.
I like the country where I was born because Brunei is a beautiful country.
That's all about my country.

ABDEL HADI, 10

* Subdistrict of Brunei

Negera Brunei Darussalam

Saya tinggal di Negara Brunei Darussalam. Saya suka negeri saya. Pada masa cuti saya selalu bermain bola. Setiap negeri mesti mespunyai bendera. saya seorang budak Islam.

Saya tinggal di Berakas, Warna bendera negeri saya ialah kuning, merah, hitam dan putih. Saya suka warna biru. Saya suka makan nasi ayam dan minum milo ping. Saya selalu ke pantai. Saya bersekolah di Bakti Dewa.

Saya suka Brunei Darussalam kerana Brunei Darussalam ialah cantik dan tempat saya di lahirkan. Begitulah cerita Negara Brunei Darussalam.

Bulgaria | Europe

We speak Bulgarian. • We eat *moussaka* (eggplant and lamb casserole) and *tarator* (cucumber-and-yogurt soup). • We play soccer and we like hiking.

NELI, 6

My Bulgaria is the best
I have four dreams:
To make a clone between a dinosaur
and a white tiger
To fly among the other birds with my
own wings
To be an astronomer and discover life
and other plants in space
To become a famous fashion designer
And with all these dreams, I hope
Bulgaria will be as proud of me
As I am proud of her.

LORA, 11

My Bălgaria
is the best.
Моите мечти са четири:
да осъществя клонинг с
динозавър и бял тигер;
Да летя сред други-
те птици с крила;
Да стана астроном
и да открия извъне
мен живот в космо-
са; И да стана из-
вестна модна дизай-
нерка.
Всичко това надявам
се България да се
гордее с мен както аз
се гордея с нея.

Burkina Faso | Africa

We speak Mooré, Dioula, Fulfuldé, and Gurmantchéma. • We eat *tô* (hard porridge) and grilled lamb. • We play soccer, and we like cycling and boxing.

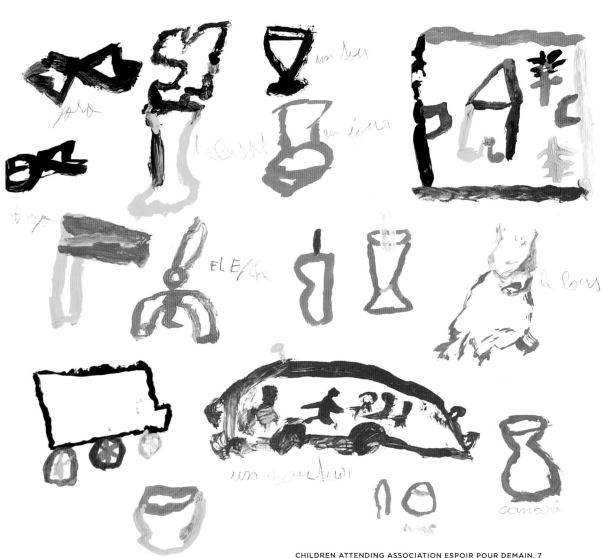

CHILDREN ATTENDING ASSOCIATION ESPOIR POUR DEMAIN, 7

In Bobo

Children are playing in the yard
Eric loves to eat papaya and melon
Bassiratou loves to eat caterpillars
Mohamed is washing his bicycle
Paul likes cows
Rebecca rides a horse
In Alima's yard you can find canaries
Bienvenu likes pigs
Saiba doesn't fear crocodiles
Marie Ange is playing with the elephants
Ibrahim feeds the rabbits
And all of this takes place under the shadow of the trees.

SAFIATOU, NAAB, AND BOURIMA, 7

A Bobo

Denmisin jouent dans la cour
Eric cume les papayes et les melons
Bassiratou aime manger les 'chitoumous'
Mhamed lave son velo
Paul aime les boeufs
Rebieca monte sur le seo
Dans la cour d'Alima, on trouve les canaris
Bienvenu aime les cocatis
Saïba n'a pas peur des hambos
Marie vinge joue avec les samas
Ibrahim nourril les sonsonnis
et Tout cela à l'ombre des yiris..

66

Burundi | Africa

We speak Kirundi and French. • We eat sweet potatoes, bananas, and *ugali* (a stiff dough eaten with sauce and vegetables). • We play soccer.

Oh my country Burundi
How beautiful it is!
With its harmonious nature
His sweet tasting flowers
All this greenery
That fulfills your heart
With all those beautiful banana trees
Oh my country Burundi
Its beautiful lakes
Like the Tanganika
With its multicolored birds
And its beautiful and fat pet animals
Oh my country Burundi,
I like it so much.

BÉNI MUHIZI, 11

Oh! mon pays le Burundi
qu'il est beau
avec toute l'harmonieuse nature
avec ses fleurs qui ont un goût sucré
avec toute cette verdure
qui rend le coeur joyeux
avec tous ses beaux bananiers.

Oh! mon pays le Burundi
avec ses beaux lacs
comme le lac Tanganyika.
avec tous ses oiseaux multicolores
avec tous ses domestiques beaux et gras.
Oh! mon pays le burundi, je l'adore tant.

QUINTIA IRADUKUNDA, 11

68

Cambodia

Asia

We speak Khmer. • We eat soup or rice for every meal, sometimes with fish, vegetables, or spicy broth. • We play soccer, table tennis, and volleyball.

Dew in the morning
Makes leaves of trees
Become green and fresh.
The wind blows softly
The birds are playing happily
Farmers harvest in the rice field,
Rice is ripe
They look happy:
The crops are good!

PRORN THAVITH, 12

CHIN VIDA, 11

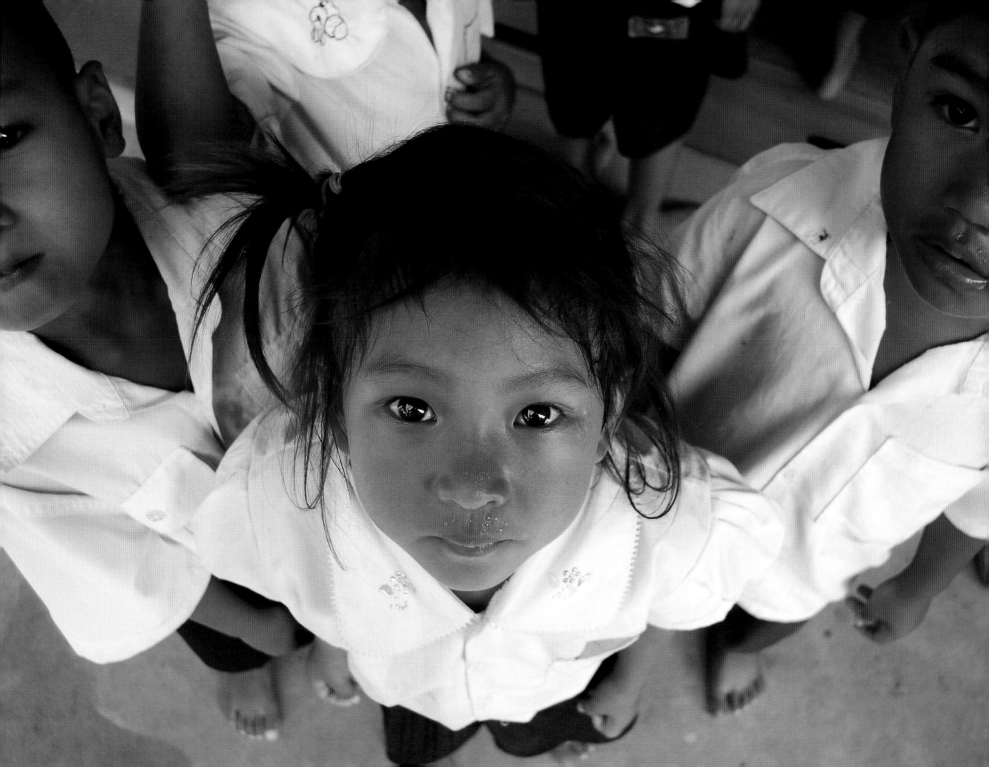

Cameroon | Africa

We speak many languages, but the official languages are French and English. • We eat *ndolé* (stew with leaves, peanuts, and fish). • We play soccer.

MAIRA MOUBOUBOU, 11

My Beautiful Village

You can find anything in my village
There are markets, gamba fields, corn, and potato …
Anything … Going to my village, you will find
Trees, houses, children walking on the road.
In my village, you will find millet, rice, corn
When you cross the road in my village,
You must look at your left,
You must look at your right.
You can find millet on the mountains,
You can find corn, gombo*, potato, and macabo**
There are so many things in my village!

CLARISSE, 11

* Green tropical vegetable also called okra
** Tuber

Mon beau village.

dans mon village tu dois trouve tout
dans mon village il y a des marché
le champ de gamba, le maïs, la patate.
tout tu peux dans mon village aussi
tu dois trouve des arbes, les maison
les enfant marche sur la route
dans mon village culture, le mil
le riz, maïs ne marcheant sur
la route de mon village tu regarde a
gauche et à drait tu regarde à gauche
tu peux trouve le mil le montagnes
le maïs et à drait tu peut trouve
le gamba, la patate, le macabo
il y a beaucoup des choses dans mon
village.

72

Canada | North America

We speak English and French. • We eat seafood, caribou, and *poutine* (french fries with gravy and cheese curds). • We play ice hockey and lacrosse.

Canada is wide and big
Not too skinny like a twig
Canada has leaves and snow
With maple syrup, whoa!!
The flag is red and white
Those 2 colors all unite

Canada is safe and free
Also with schools with students like grade 3
We have phrases like "Eh?" or "Cool!"
We also have mini pools
We have multicultural people
We also have books with different sequels
We love Canada, oh yes we do
Come and join, you can have some fun too

KRYSTAL CABICO, 10

Canada is wide and big
Not to skinny like a twig
Canada has leaves and snow
With maple syrup, Whoa!!
The flag is red and white
Those 2 colours all unite

Canada is safe and free
Also with schools with students like grade 3
We have Phrases like Eh? or Cool!
We also have mini Pools
We have multi cultural people
We also have books with different sequels
We love Canada Oh yes we do
Come and join you can have some fun to

AUTUMN FRENCH, 10

74

Cape Verde | Africa

We speak Portuguese and Crioulo. • We eat a lot of rice and beans, often served with fish or pork, and *cachupa* (corn stew). • We play soccer.

Cabo Verde

Quiet country
Full of trees and birds.

Little rain
Lots of love.

10 grains spread
In the ocean.

Little wealth.
A lot of peace.

ANA PAULA, 10

Mountainous islands
Flat islands
Uncommon islands.

PREMISE, 10

Central African Republic | Africa

We speak Sango and French. • We eat a variety of fruits, including bananas, guavas, pineapples, and mangoes. • We play soccer and basketball.

Central Africa, my beautiful country
Why are you suffering?
You, who have so many varieties
Of the fortunes of the world
You have the Oubangui river,

That contains fish, hippopotamus,
oysters, and caymans
Your forest is full of different animals
Your trees and plants have so many uses:
House, furniture, medicine, aliments

In your soil we find diamonds, iron, gold, oil, and cement
You have many fields
I hope to see one day
All the children in unity
Working and caring for the progress of our country
Central Africa I love you.

BADO IRENEE, 11

GBOUTET ARIELLE, 11

Centrafrique mon beau pays
porquoi souffre tu?

Toi qui as beaucoup de variété
de richesse du monde.
Tu as le fleuve oubangui qui
contient, les poissons, les hippopotams
les huitre caïmants etc...
Tu as la forêt plein de different
sorte d'animaux
Tes arbres et les plants sont utiles
à beaucoup des choses : Maisons
meubles, medicaments, nourriture...
on trouve dans ta terre, les diamants
le fer, l'or, le petrole, ciment...
Tu as plusieurs terrains de champ.
J'espere un jour a nous voir les
enfants dans l'unité.
Dans le souci d'evoluer tous
de travailler d'avantage pour le
progres de notre pays
centrafrique je t'aime

78

Chad | Africa

We speak French, Arabic, and other languages. • We eat *boule* (porridge balls), dried fish, goat, and tropical fruits. • We play soccer and basketball.

sou dou dague
M, yidi sou dou dague
Minas ti soudou dague
M! ndonder soudou dague
Mibel nounde densoudou

dague

I love my straw house
For in this straw house
I feel relaxed

KELOU BOURDAMSOU, 11

I would always like to see the Chari,
River of Chad
that runs in the morning and in the evening
Toward Lake Chad
Where I take my animals to drink.

ADAM ABANOUR, 11

Bingel, nomad
mila takl bingell django delhald
nomad mani kossam
mi dali marle abba djeam gan
mi waro
hae cob
to mi waniec lo mi django, mi vvi
nda
mi wadda doorgolboodoummi
naro
djamou dou nia

I am a student of the nomad school of Mani Kossam
I abandoned my parents' cattle to come to school.
For at school, I will learn: to read and write, to have
a modern livestock,
And to have good health.

ADAM ABDOULAYE, 11

MAHAMAT IDRISS, 9

Chile | South America

We speak Spanish. • We eat *empanadas de horno* (meat turnovers), *cazuela de ave* (chicken soup), and seafood. • We play soccer and basketball.

My City

Ice city
In between the snowed points of the mountains
I sharpen my ear and hear
The whisper, the wind and birds
there on the top the wind roars

Lower, my enchanted city
by the population and the streets
but the cutest thing is the green of the trees
and the sound of the lakes and rivers
when the snow has retreated

the snowman has been left behind
and the crystalized water pond
the woolen clothes are put away
and they wait for the spring to go out and take a walk
down the green and blossoming prairie
and the birds sing and the butterflies dance
and look forward the beauty of my city

MARÍA SANTANA LLEUFU, 10

EVELYN DELGADO, 13

82

China | Asia

We speak many languages, but mostly Mandarin. • We eat noodle dishes, rice, *jiaozi* (Chinese dumplings), and duck. • We play soccer and table tennis.

The Four Seasons in the Village

Peach blossoms smile in Spring;
Frogs sing in Summer;
Fruits jump in Autumn;

Calyx canthus wakes up in Winter.
This is the four seasons in our village.
How lovely they are!

When I grow up
I may go somewhere far away,
but I will never forget my home village,
with the pure and sincere love to my hometown.

LI YUANYUAN, 10

LIU HONGYING, 10

Colombia | South America

We speak Spanish. • We eat *empanadas* (meat turnovers), *arroz con pollo* (chicken with rice), and *arepas* (cornmeal pancakes). • We play soccer.

DAVID AGUIRRE, 11

Colombia is a flower
Colombia is divine like the sun
Like the heavenly sky
Like a tree
Like a chocolate bar
Colombia you are a honey moon
You are the bright stars
You are the white cloud covering our sky
Colombia, little ray of light
Colombia is my country
Where I was born

XIMENA GODOY MENIDIVIL, 10

colombia es como una flor
colombia es divino como el sol
como el cielo divino
como un arbol
como un chocomani's
colombia eres luna de mi
eres luceros en cencido
eres nube blanca que cobre
nuestro cielo
colombia rasiso de loß
colombia es mi Rais
donde to nici

Comoros | Africa

We speak French and Arabic. • We eat a lot of fish and rice, as well as a variety of fruits. • We play soccer, basketball, and volleyball.

The Comoros

They are four volcanic islands
Four magnificent islands
In the Indian Ocean
Where the Comorians live

Four islands of perfumes
Where jasmine grows
Ylang ylang* and beautiful fruits
And plenty of birds

These beaches and their fine sand
So glistening and so attractive
We dream of happiness
And warm our heart

Their salt lake and the bright moon
With a thousand twinkling sparkles
Give us courage to go for a walk
Every evening with a beautiful smile
And many roars of laughter.

NOURAYNAT HASSAN, 10

*Tropical tree with sweet-scented flowers, used in perfumery

LAMYAT BACAR, 11

Comores

Ce sont quatre îles volcaniques
Quatre îles ~~sont~~ magnifiques
Dans l'Océan Indien
Où vivent les Comorien

Quatre îles aux parfums
Où poussent le Jasmin
L'ylang ylang, et de beaux fruits
Avec de multiples oiseaux

Les plage et leurs sables fin
Si brillant et si attirant
Nous font rêver de bonheur et
Nous réchauffent le cœur

Leur lac salé et la lune brillante
Aux mille étincelles scintillantes
Nous donnent le courage de nous promener
Tous les soirs avec un beau sourire
Et beaucoup d'éclats de rire

Congo (Democratic Republic) | Africa

We speak Lingala, Kikongo, Tshiluba, Swahili, and French. • We eat rice, potatoes, bananas, yams, bean, fish, and chicken. • We play soccer.

KAMBALA ORNELLA, 11

MON pays la RDC.

je pile le pondu

j'mange le kaleji

je prepare le matamba

je donne les chenilles à mes freres

j'aime les haricots

la maison de ma mère est en briques

j'aime mon ecole.

ma tante fait la griculture

mon frère et ma soeur joue au foot ball

ma tante achète un vélo

mon frère achète le pain

chaque matin je brosse les dents
j'aime étudier à la maison.

chaque fois je dors à la maison

je balaye la maison chaque jours

je mes laves chaques matin

je joue avec le poupé

j fait la lessive je lave le chemisere et le pantalons

faire la vaisselle laver les assiettes

je fabrique des voitwe en fille

je tresse le cheveux a la maison

je respecte mon père. j'aime aider ma mère si travailler

I pound the pondu*

I eat kaleji*

I cook matamba*

I give the caterpillars to my brothers

I like beans.

My mother's house is made of bricks.

I like my school.

My aunt farms.

My brother and my sister play football.

My aunt buys a bicycle.

My brother buys bread

Every morning I brush my teeth

I like to study at home

I always sleep at home

I sweep out the house every day

I wash myself every day

And I play with my doll

I do the laundry I wash shirt and trousers

Wash the dishes, wash the plates

I make cars out of wire

I braid my hair at home

I respect my father

I like to help my mother to work.

MULUMBA JEMIMAH, 11

* Dishes made out of cassava leaves, pounded in a mortar

Congo (Republic) | Africa

We speak many languages, but our official language is French.   •   We eat potatoes, yams, plantains, rice, and fish.   •   We play soccer.

Mon pays a 2 grandes saisons
la saison des pluies et la saison
sèche Certains préfèrent l'une ou
l'autre saison
moi je les adore toutes
la saison de pluie fait pousser les
cultures et nous pouvons manger à notre
faim la saison sèche permet aux
agriculteurs de débroussaillé des
champs aussi de sécher leurs
récoltes.

My land has two important seasons
The rainy season and the dry season.
Some prefer one season or another
But I love them both
The rainy season makes the crops grow
And we can eat our fill
The dry season lets the farmers
Weed the fields
And dry their harvests.

KINKELA JOLDA, 10

NKENDA BALOKI, 10

Costa Rica | Central America

We speak Spanish. • We eat rice and beans at most meals. • We play a variety of sports, but soccer is the most popular.

Se le llama hermosura
al esplendor de Costa Rica
con bosques lluviosos
y playas de arena blanca

Lo que yo más quiero
son los bailes y tradiciones
como "El diablito" y las leyendas
que tanto llegan a los corazones

La riqueza natural
aquí es lo más especial
como los volcanes
y todos los animales

Costa Rica es más bonita
de lo que pude describir
pero tengo que decir.
adiós, me tengo que ir.

The splendor of Costa Rica
Is called beauty
With rainy forests
And white sandy beaches.

What I love the most
Are the dances and traditions
Like the dance of the "devils"* and legends
That touch so deeply the people's hearts

The natural richness
Is the most special here
Like the volcanoes
And all the animals.

Costa Rica is more beautiful
Than what I can describe
Yet I have to say goodbye,
I have to go.

CHRYSTELL VIQUEZ CAMPOS, 12

*Tradition where the devils represent native people fighting against Spanish conquerors

SEBASTIAN HIDALGO VARGAS, 7

Cote d' Ivoire | Africa

We speak many languages, but our official language is French. • We eat rice, porridge, and tropical fruits. • We play soccer and *dame* (checkers).

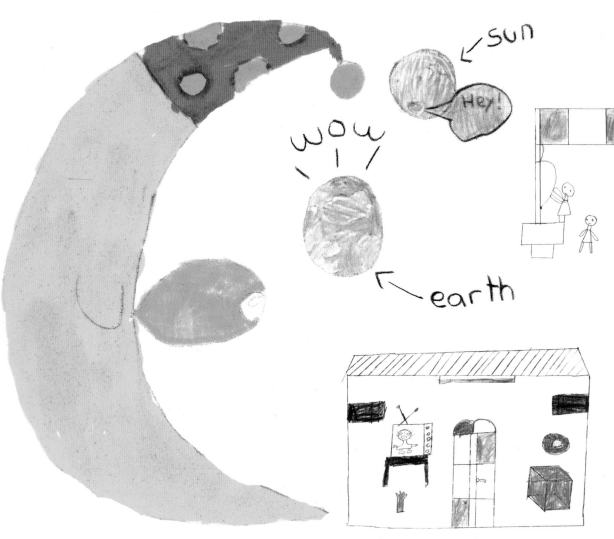

NABAGATE BARAKISSA, 10

What is this feeling that is said
to be sometimes stronger than love,
and that can live in each of us
until the end of times.
What is this hand that leans toward
you and that is still here when
everything goes wrong.
This is love from Ivory Coast.

TOURE IBRAHIM, 9

Quel est ce sentiment que l'on dit
parfois plus fort que l'amour et
qui peut vivre en chacun de nous
jusqu'à la fin des jours
quelle est cette main qui se tend vers
toi et qui est encore là quand tout va
mal . c'est l'amour de la côte d-ivoire

Croatia | Europe

We speak Croatian. • We eat chicken, beef, fish, pork, and lamb, and *štrukli* (cheese dumplings). • We play soccer, basketball, handball, and water polo.

KATHRINA STANCIC, 10

I live in the most beautiful country in the world
It's called Croatia.
It has landscapes, mountains, and sea.
Zagreb is the capital city.
Croatia has many towns, islands, and villages.
Everyday she's prettier and prettier …
Bigger and bigger …
I like her very much.
And those who come here,
Will like her too.

IVA HODAK, 10

Moja država Hrvatska
Ja živim u najljepšoj državi na
svijetu koja se zove Hrvatska. Ona ima
brežuljke, planine, more i ravnicu. Njen
glavni grad je Zagreb. Hrvatska ima
brojne gradove, otoke i sela. Hrvatska
je svakim danom sve ljepša i ljepša i,
sve veća i veća. Ja ju jako
volim i onaj koji ovamo u nju
dovodit će ju.

Cuba | Central America

We speak Spanish. • We eat *arroz y frijoles* (rice and beans), *boniatos* (sweet potatoes), and tropical fruits. • We play baseball and basketball.

A Tribute to My Valley

Beautiful valley, green and warm,
Your perfumed fragrances,
Tune after tune,
Enrapture us sweetly
And take us to our cradles
With a clef, a guitar, and a drum,
Bringing joy to our hearts in an eternal delusion
Which turns men into children
And gives the elderly hope.

FLAVIA PEREZ, 9

ÁNGEL LUIS AND ELVIS LÓPEZ, 10

"Homenaje a mi Valle"
Valle hermoso, verde y tibio,
de fragancias perfumadas,
son que tras cada tonada
nos embriaga de dulzura,
llevándonos hasta la cuna
con clave, guitarra y tambor,
alegrando el corazón en un
eterno delirio,
que vuelve al hombre niño
y al anciano da ilusión.

Cyprus | Europe

We speak Greek and Turkish. • We eat *fasolada* (white beans), pork, chicken, lamb, olives, and hummus. • We play soccer, volleyball, and tennis.

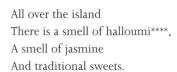

HERCULES PELIVANIDES, 12

Here is Cyprus,
A land of sea and sun,
Of Salamina* and Tefkros**,
Of ancient sites like Kitium and Zenon***.

Here is Cyprus,
Where every piece of land is a legend,
Where every path is a monument,
The whole island is a big museum.

Here is Cyprus,
With traditions and activities.
Feasts and dances
Are always lively.

All over the island
There is a smell of halloumi****,
A smell of jasmine
And traditional sweets.

Here is Cyprus,
The island of Venus,
The daughter of our friendly Zeus.
That's why everybody is friendly.

Here is Cyprus,
The wounded homeland
Asking consistently
For freedom.

ERINEOS AGATHAGGELOU, 12

* Ancient city state
** Greek king who founded Salamina
*** Philosopher born in Kitium, now called Larnaca
**** Goat and sheep milk cheese

Czech Republic | Europe

We speak Czech. • We eat bread dumplings, goulash, sauerkraut, sausages, and potatoes. • We play ice hockey, and we like camping and hiking.

Czech Republic,
Our country,
Our homeland,
A beauty to the eyes,
We don't have beaches nor sea
But we don't mind
We have Chevrolet

And even great Ferraris
Passing by our streets,
Going here and there.
And I'm already waiting here for one of them
I'll go nuts
And then I will go on the footpath

PETR KRATOCHVI AND JAN VASTECHVSKY, 10

VERONIKA TABORIKOVA, 10

Denmark | Europe

We speak Danish. • We eat pumpernickel bread and *frikadeller* (hamburger steak with fried onions). • We play soccer, handball, and badminton.

THEA FISKER, 9

The Beautiful Country

Summer winter
The sun the snow
Flowers growing in the wild
Because Denmark is my country
The snow there is so beautiful
On the good soil
The scent of the beautiful grass
Makes me crazy
And the beautiful sea
Shines like real
Gold

SUKAENA AKTAM, 9

Det smukke land
Sommer vinter
Solen sneen
blomster Der vokser i naturen
fordi Danmark er mit land
Sneen der er så smuk.
på den gode jord
duften af det smukke græs
gør mig skør
og det smukke hav
skinner som ægte
guld

Djibouti | Africa

We speak French, Arabic, Somali, and Afar. • We eat rice, seafood, and *looho* (thin pancake-like food). • We play soccer and *pétanque* (lawn bowling).

HOUDA MOHAMED HASSAN, 10

I love my country Djibouti
I thank my mother for coming from here
In my country there is no rain
But there are fish and night fishing
You lose your mind when you see our sea
The beach, the fisherman, and my brothers
I love Djibouti and I could never stray far
There is no war and no casualties here
I love Djibouti and the Aïd* festivals
I love the people and the traffic jams
I love Djibouti and will remain here

MARWA AHMED HAGUI, 10

* Muslim celebrations

J'aime mon pays Djibouti.
Je remercie ma mère d'être ici.
Dans mon pays, il n'y a de pluie.
Mais on a le poisson et la pêche de nuit.
Tu perds la tête quand tu vois les mers,
les   , plages, les pêcheurs et les frères.
J'aime Djibouti et je ne peux pas m'éloigner,
car il n'y a de pas guerre, ni des blessés.
J'aime Djibouti, les jours de la Ide.
J'aime les gens et les embouteillages.
Je aime Djibouti et je resterai ici.

108

Dominica | Central America

We speak English. • We eat a lot of seafood, including tuna, marlin, ballyhoo, and crayfish, and a variety of tropical fruits. • We play soccer and cricket.

SHERLIN BARON, 9

Dominica

Imagine an island
So beautiful and majestic
Magnificent with big green mountains
365 rivers roaring down to the sea
Wonderful waterfalls
Fun filled black beaches
And lovely people
Full of culture and tradition

This is Dominica, my beautiful island

SHAHEEDA HENDERSON, 9

Dominica

Imagine an island
So beautiful and majestic
Magnificent with big green mountains
365 rivers roaring down to the sea
Wonderful waterfalls
Fun filled black beaches
And lovely people
Full of culture and tradition

This is Dominica my beautiful island

Dominican Republic | Central America

We speak Spanish. • We eat rice and beans at most meals, fruit, and *sancocho* (a vegetable-and-meat stew). • We play baseball and basketball.

JOMAIRA VELASQUEZ MATEO, 13

My flag has three colors
I respect it so much
My country has so much culture
Pretty flowers
Wonderful people
Everyone look at us, wherever we go!
How beautiful is my country
How beautiful is my land
How beautiful are the flowers of my country
Because we are Dominican

MARIA YESSENIA PEREZ SALDANA, 15

Mi bandera es tricolor
La respeto muchisimo
mi pais tiene mucha cultura
Flores agradable personas
maravillosa donde llegamos
todos nos miran.

Que lindo es mi pais
Que linda es mi tierra
Que linda son la flores
de mi tierra.

ya que somos
Dominicano

Ecuador | South America

We speak Spanish and Kichwa. • We eat soup at most meals, corn, potatoes, and *fritada* (fried pork). • We play soccer and Ecuadorian volleyball.

Mi País Ecuador

Hermosura en tus campos conservas
laureles pinos y palmas
ríos nevados y mares
costa, sierra, Oriente y galápagos
indios, (cholos), negros mestizos
adornan a mi noble país Ecuador

No hay duda te sobra grandeza
tierra excelsa de héroes, músicos
poetas escritores y políticos
tus hombres y mujeres llenos
de valor esfuerzo trabajo
jardín de belleza sin fin

tiene ríos nevados volcanes
reptiles manglares, jaguares
que alzan blanco mare,
hecho cúspide andina
los ríos caminan para dar
verdor y hermosura
a mi querido país Ecuador

tierra de árboles, cáctus
minas, petroleo, madera
llanura valles y lagunas
la extensión de tu campo
nada existe más bello
que mi país Ecuador

ANALY PAVÓN, 12

My Country Ecuador

Beauty you keep in your countryside
Laurels, pines, and palm trees,
Rivers, snowy mountains, and seas
Coast, mountain range, east, and Galápagos
Indians, Andeans, blacks, people of mixed race
Decorate my noble country Ecuador.

There is no doubt of your abundant grandeur
Lofty land of heroes, musicians,
Poets, writers, and politicians
Your men and women filled
with courage, effort, work,
Garden of endless beauty.

You have rivers, snow-covered peaks, volcanoes
Reptiles, mangroves, jaguars
That raise white seas,
Made Andean peaks,
The rivers walk just to walk
To see smell and beauty
Of my beloved country Ecuador.

Land of trees, cactus,
Mines, petroleum, wood,
Plains, valleys, and lakes
The extent of your countryside
Nothing more beautiful exists
Than my country Ecuador.

GUILLERMO CHANGÚN, 10

Egypt | Africa

We speak Arabic and Nubian.   •   We eat rice, bread, fish, lamb, chicken, fava beans, and stuffed vegetables.   •   We play soccer.

STUDENTS OF AL TALEE BEENAGEE KHAYREYA SCHOOL, 10

Egypt

Egypt, the land of the Nile
    It holds all civilization
Its beautiful weather
        And its rich land
It has security and safety
        It has love and compassion
The Nile flows in it
        Clear and calm
The blessed land
        And safety and security
It holds civilization
    Its skies are clear
The land of mosques
        It has green land.

MOHAMED BEKHIT ABOU EL FADL, 12

مصر

مصر أرض النيل
تملك كل الحضاره
بجوها الجميل
وأرضها الخصبة
فيها الأمن والأمان
فيها الحب والحنان

مصارى النيل
صافيا هادئا
أرض الخير
والأمن والأمان
تملك الحضاره
سماها صافيه
أرض المآذن
فيها الأراضى الخضراء

El Salvador | Central America

We speak Spanish. • We eat *frijoles* (red beans), rice, fruit, and tortillas stuffed with meat, beans, or cheese. • We play soccer, basketball, and softball.

ALISSON GOMEZ NIETO, 10

Mountains, Volcanoes, and Lakes from El Salvador

Oh! What beautiful
Mountains, volcanoes, and lakes
From my Salvador, I ask
That my wish were fulfilled.

That they were alive
And that they were my friends,
To always play with me,
Every single day of my life.

Mountains, volcanoes, and lakes
It is like saying 1,2,3, or
Red, Blue, and Yellow and
I love you so dearly.

JORGE ERNESTO GRANADOS, 11

CERROS, VOLCANES Y LAGOS DE EL SALVADOR

¡Oh! qué Lindos LOS
Cerros, volcanes y Lagos
DE Mi Salvador, Un deseo
pidiera qué fuera.

Qué tuvieran vida y
fueran mis amigos,
para jugar siempre conmigo,
todos los días de mi vida.

Cerros, volcanes y Lagos
es como decir 1,2,3 o
Rojo, Azul y amarillo, y
Yo te quiero con mucho cariño.

Equatorial Guinea | Africa

We speak French and Pidgin English, but our official language is Spanish.   •   We eat goat, chicken, fish, and tropical fruits.   •   We play soccer.

JACINTA NGONO NGUEMA, 12

The flag of Equatorial Guinea is the most beautiful
in the world.
That's why it has four colors: green, white, red, and blue
Green means that Guinea has many riches from the
forests and from agriculture;
If we chop down a tree we must plant new ones;
We must cultivate more farms, not to lose all this wealth.
White means that we are good to our neighbors, to
our families, and that we do not have trouble with other
countries …
… that we live in peace
Red reminds us that Guineans have died defending the
independence
Blue is the color of the sky and the sea uniting the lands.

MARIA DEL ROSARIO MANGUE EBENDENG OCONO, 12

La Bandera de Guinea ecuatorial es la más bella y hermosa
del mundo. Por eso dispone de cuatro colores que son verde
blanco rojo y azul;

El verde quiere decir que Guinea tiene mucha riqueza del bos-
que y de la agricultura si cortamos un arbol debemos
plantar otros más nuevos para no perder esa riqueza
debemos cultivar más fincas.

El color blanco quiere decir que estamos bien con nuestros
vecinos, con las familiares que no tenemos problemas con
otros países que vivimos en paz.
El color rojo nos recuerda que los Guineanos han muerto por
defender a la indepedencia.

El color azul es el color del cielo y también es el color
del mar que une las tierras.

120

Eritrea | Africa

We speak Tigrinya, Arabic, and English. • We eat spicy meat dishes with *ingera* (sour pancake bread) and drink very strong coffee. • We play soccer.

How beautiful is her land
How resourceful are her ports
How mild is her weather,
She welcomes guests with happiness
Her three seasons come in two hours
God created her in a good place
Food is harvested from her mountains and fields
Salt is harvested from her Red Sea
Thanks to God who provided us with all this.

SOLIANA TEKESTE, 8

BANA MUSSIE, 10

ሰሳይና ተከስተ ተከፈይዋ
ክፋሕ 3ፊ ዕመፅ 8 ዩተ ነ
ክንደዒሁ ዷዶነኝ ኊቲ መሲዓ
ንዖመ ክመቶቈሰ ኊቲ መዷሰተ፡
ክዖርኢ ንዖፈዖኢ ኊዖ መዐዷ ኊፈ ነዖሠደ
ዓንዛ ገዕ ሰዐታጎ ዷቈሰኢዖ
ክሰተ ኊጒዖዓቶ ክሰተ መዷሰፈዖ
ኊዖሰኝ ኊሰ ቅሰቈ ሰቲ ሰሬተዖ፡፡
ጋሰተዖና ዐዷተፈዖ ኊፈሰ ሰኝፈዖ
ቀዷኢ ሰኊርፈና መዐዖ ሰኝፈዖ
ኊዖሰኝ ዷመ፡ገገ ንፈዖ ሰክገ፡

122

Estonia | Europe

We speak Estonian. • We eat dark rye bread, fish, wild berries, and *rosolje* (pink potato salad). • We play basketball and volleyball.

There is one beautiful country
That is Estonia
Estonia is my homeland
There, I want to be!

MARGO RODI, 10

ON ÜKS ILUS MAA
SEE ON EESTIMAA.
EESTIMAA ON MINU KODUMAA
SEAL MA TAHAN OLLA

My homeland isn't small
In summertime there is rain and thunder
But the sun is shining

TANEL KIISLA, 8

MU ISAMAA
POLE VÄIKE,
SUVEL ON
SIIN VIHM JA
ÄIKE KUID
SIIS JÄLLE PAISTAB
PÄIKE

TAAVI MEINBERG, 9

Ethiopia | Africa

We speak many languages, but Amharic is our official language. • We eat *ingera* (sour pancake bread) and drink coffee. • We play *gena* (field hockey).

Ethiopia, the country we love
Our mother country, where we live
The green, yellow, and red flag
The green meadows we see are nice
And comfortable to roll around
The genfo* and kitfo** eaten with butter
Are as yummy as a jar of honey

When we dance in our traditional clothes
When the coffee boils and we eat injera***
And we drink our tej**** and tela*****
When Abebe Bekila runs barefoot
He wins a race and makes history
When the athlete Tirunesh runs she makes us happy
She makes Ethiopia known in other countries

When the athlete Haile Giselassie runs he looks like a lion
Whenever he runs, he stands for his honor
The country where many people are found
This is Ethiopia, the place we live in.
Long live Ethiopia!

BEZAWIT WORKEYE & RAKEB MEGBAR, 10

* Barley porridge
** Raw minced meat
*** Flat pancake made of cereals fermented in water
**** Honey beer
***** Sorghum beer

EDEN KEBEDE, 10

ጉንፍኦ ኮተፍኦ

እንደ ህገረን የእዉመወሰጠን ኮተፍኦ
ጉፍ ህገረን ዓ ሬ መ ዋሬፍ
ኽሬንጀዉ ብሜ ቀፍ ለእ ዩኦፍ3ን
የጉተፍኦይ ህንን ዩ ኽ ሰበየፍን::
ኽርጎንዉ ዉ ሻዩ ዉ ዩመረዩ ጠሰ
ለነተገ ለሰ የመያሰየጠዉ
ግንዉዉ ጉገዉ ለ ዉ ሰበ
ዓግ ሚጠ ለጠ ህ ዩ ሚ ዉ ለዩ::
ለህሰ ኽሰ ፍን ማዬዋ ሰ ዬሰ
ዩ ኽ ፍኽ ህንደ ሰ ኽሰ
ኽዬ ርገ ዩ ም ዬ ጉ ፍነ ዩ ፍን ::
ኽን ለ ሰ ለ ህ ህ ዩ ዉ ም
ኽሸዩ ገኽ ኽ ዬ መ ማ ::
ዋ ዩ ለ በ ፍ ዩ መ ዩ
የ ኽተፍ ኦ ፍን ማ ጠ ፍኽ ፍ ::
ህዩ ለ ዬ ኽ ፍ ዩ መ ዋ ኽ ፍ
መ ዬ ለ ዉ ኽ ለ ዩ ዋ ::
የ ፍ ም ም ዬ ዩ መ ዉ ለ ዉ
ዬ ዉ ዬ ኽተፍ ፍ ዬ ፍ መ ዉ ፍ::

Fiji

Oceania

We speak Fijian and Hindustani, but our official language is English.   •   We eat seafood and many tropical fruits.   •   We play rugby, soccer, and cricket.

MICHELLE LEE, 13

My Beautiful Island

My island on the map
Is just a little tiny dot
A little inky spot
Near the corner of a page.

But if you come and see my country
With trees and birds and colorful sights
You might wanna stay forever
And be a part of my weather.

My country Fiji, a beautiful place
To come and relax and see the face
On the burning west where the sun sets
Is where I live and is the best.

POLLY VATU, 13

My island on the map
Is just a little tiny dot
A little inky spot
Near the corner of a page

But if you come and see my country
With trees and birds and colourful sights
You might wanna stay forever
And be apart of my weather

My country Fiji a beautiful place
To come and relax and see the face
On the burning west where the sun sets
Is where I live and is the best

Finland | Europe

We speak Finnish and Swedish. • We eat seafood, reindeer, wild berries, and *makkara* (sausage). • We play ice hockey and *pesäpallo* (baseball).

FUNNY SATURDAY CHILDREN

The land of Finland is the best land
there are many great things in Finland
Farm animals, yellow fields, and blue lakes.

The Finns are lazy and quiet,
they are also wise
The Finns make toys
and get good praise.

Santa Claus is also here,
Living in the northern sphere
Midsummer is a nightless night
when the mosquitoes like to bite.

FUNNY SATURDAY CHILDREN

Suomen maa on paras maa
Suomessa on monta hyvää asiaa
Maatilan eläimet, keltaiset pellot, siniset järvet.
Suomalaiset ovat laiskoja ja hiljaisia,
he ovat myös viisaita.
Suomalaiset tekevät leluja
ja saavat hyviä kehuja.
Täällä asuu myös Joulupukki,
Joka on Pohjoisen asukki.
Juhannus on yötön yö,
Jolloin hyttyset syö.

France | Europe

We speak French. • We eat *croque-monsieurs* (ham-and-cheese sandwiches) and snails. • We play soccer, rugby, and *pétanque* (lawn bowling).

Rhymes From My Country

In Paris they finish the rice
In Toulouse cows live in the grass
In Aubervilliers there are firefighters
In Marseille there are bees
In Nice they make spiced bread
In Nantes they make mint
In Monaco there are coconuts
In Nancy all the cats are grey
In La Courneuve all the cars are new
In Sarcelle they play cellos

MATTHIEU, 8

Les rumes de mon pays

À Paris on finit le riz
à Toulouse les vaches vivent sur la pelouse
à Aubervilliers il y a des pompiers
à Marseille il y a des abeilles
à Nice on fait des pain d'épice
à Nantes on fait de la menthe
à Monaco y des noix de coco
à Nancy tous les chats sont gris
à La Courneuve toutes les voitures sont neuves
à Sarcelle on fait du violoncelle

RADOUANE, 11

Gabon | Africa

We speak French. • We eat rice, fish, *piment* (hot peppers), tropical fruits, and some wild animals. • We play soccer, basketball, and volleyball.

You Gabon

You are a holy land
When your rivers flow
I am very happy
If I could hold you in my arms one day
My Gabon you are a rich land, Gabon !

You are a tiny continent in Africa
Whom I love
When I see your colors
I describe Gabon
The earth turns
The years pass

The ancestors return
The seawind blows
And the water moves with joy when it sees
Gabon
It's as if I see a shining star
Fallen from the sky

The pure white clouds praising
Gabon
You love peace and joy
I love that proverb from Gabon
You will anchor your sea
Before fixing me fast.

MIHINDOU CLEVIS, 11

POUABOU JUNIOR, 11

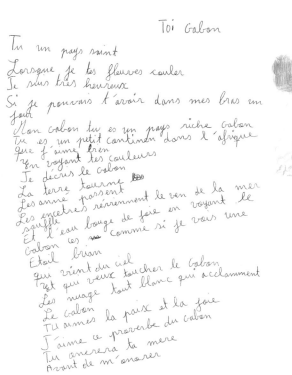

Toi Gabon

Tu un pays saint
Lorsque je tes fleuves couler
Je suis très heureux
Si je pouvais t'avoir dans mes bras un jour
Mon gabon tu es un pays riche Gabon
Tu es un petit continent dans l'afrique
que j'aime bien
En voyant tes couleurs
Je décris le Gabon
La terre tourne
Les années passent
Les encetres réviennent le ven de la mer
souffle
Et l'eau bouge de joie en voyant le
Gabon es comme si je vois une
Etoil brian
qui vient du ciel
et qui veux toucher le Gabon
Les nuage tout blanc qui acclamment
Le Gabon
Tu aimes la paix et la joie
J'aime ce proverbe du Gabon
Tu anerera ta mere
Avant de m'anorer

134

Gambia | Africa

We speak English, Wolof, Mandinka, and Fula. • We eat spicy meat stews and *supakanja* (okra soup). • We play beach soccer and volleyball.

Gambia,
Land of the fiery sun
And crashing sea waves
Of the blue, blue sky
And brown patched earth
Of the flat savannah
And murky swamps

Gambia
Land of the smiling sea
And a rainbow people
Of brave sea men
And strong land women
Of hunters of heroic past
And soccer on the beach

Gambia
Land of throbbing drums
And stamping feet
Of finger-licking benachin*
And afra* and ebbeh*
Of visits under the mango trees
And midnight tales that never cease

Gambia, oh Gambia,
Long may we live together.

GIDEON ABRAHAM, 10

* Traditional Gambian dishes

GIDEON ABRAHAM, 10

Georgia | Asia

We speak Georgian. • We eat *matsoni* (mild yogurt), *khinkali* (meat dumplings), and *satsivi* (fried chicken). • We play soccer, basketball, and tennis.

IAMZE MCHEDLURI AND LUDA CHILACHAVA, 10

There is a small country
There is a small girl
There is a small place
Where there is a lot of space
For love, devotion, and belief.

There is one wish in her mind
To see her homeland again
Brightened and blossomed
She trusts the God
And prays for her wish
To come true.

EVA SHEKRILADZE, 10

ის პატარა საქართველო
არის პატარა გოგო
და არის პატარა ადგილი
ის ბევრი ადგილი აქვსთდა
ერთი თავდადებასთ მგონია
მხოლოდ ის არის ერთი
მხოლოდ ის და ესარიუბან
არის საბრძნო საქართველო
ბევრი წახან ისუპბანო
ის ნახავ თავ ისურით აისრეთ
და არ ისთავა მისი
ის ჰსიტიის თავ ისუპმისი
ქვეყანა ესერ ამისურია
თავ საგთანულება საგახ
ქვეგანატ რტავე ნახავ.

Germany | Europe

We speak German.   •   We eat noodles, dumplings, potatoes, pork, lamb, fish, *wurst* (sausage), and a wide variety of pastries.   •   We play soccer.

SERDAL AYDIN, 12

In Germany it's almost always cold
And almost always warm
In summer it is warm
In winter it is cold
In spring it rains
In autumn the leaves fall down
In summer a lot of people go
swimming
And they dress short

In winter it is cold
And people dress warm
Some play with the snow
And make a snowman
And drink hot chocolate
And sit by the chimney
In spring the flowers bleed
And get a lot of water
A lot of sun and they bloom

SERDAL AYDIN, 12

In Deuschland ist es fast
imer Kalt und fast imer
warm. im Sommer ist es
warm. im Winter ist es
Kalt. im Fröling regnets. Im
Herbst fallen die Blätter runter.
Im Somma gehen viele Meschen
ins Freibad und ziehen sich
Kurz an. Im Winter ist es
Kalt da ziehen sich die
Meschen warm an und
Manche spielen mit dem
Schnee und Macht sie einen
Schneeman und Trinken sie
Kakao und sizen am
Kamin. im Fröling blüten
die Blumen und sie krigen
viel Wasser und viel Sonne
und sie werden in ein blumen

Ghana | Africa

We speak English. • We eat yams, beans, rice, *tuo zaafi* (a thick porridge), and tropical fruits. • We play soccer, volleyball, and basketball.

orange
Oranges
Mango
Garden Egg
Tomatoes
wood house
tree
apple
mango
Pear
Orange
Sea

CHRISTINA ACQUAH, 11

Ghana is green because it has trees
Ghana is red because it has pawpaw
Ghana is yellow because it has pineapple
Ghana is green because it has orange and apple
Ghana is red because it has tomatoes
Ghana is yellow because it has mangoes
Ghana is blue and white because of peace and the ocean
Red, yellow, green has the Ghanaian flag!

ELIZABETH ANDOH, 11

Pawpaw

GHANA has Green because it has tree.
GHANA has Red because it has pawpaw.
GHANA has yellow because it has pineapple
GHANA has Green because it has orange and apple.
GHANA has Red because it has tomatoes.
GHANA has Reyellow because it has mangoes.
GHANA has blue and white because Peace and OCEN
Red, yellow, Green has GHana Flag

Greece | Europe

We speak Greek. • We eat lamb, seafood, olives, eggplant, stuffed tomatoes, and *souvlaki* (meat shish kebab). • We play soccer and basketball.

The sky is light blue
The sea is blue
The trees are green.
Where do I live?
I live in Greece!
Where the sea is big,
And the land is small.
It's the most beautiful country in the world
It's our Greece.

ELEN LABROBOULOU, 12

Ο ουρανός γαλάζιος,
η θάλασσα μπλε,
τα δέντρα ολοπράσινα,
πού ζω;
Μα, στην Ελλάδα ζω.
Εκεί που η θάλασσα.
είναι μεγάλη
μικρή δη χωριό
Στη πιο όμορφη
χώρα στο κόσμο

Στην Ελλάδα ΜΑΣ.

FOTINI PAPALEONIDOPOULOU, 13

144

Grenada | Central America

We speak English. • We eat plantains, rice, peas, seafood, mangoes, coconuts, and *dahl* (curried chickpeas). • We play cricket, soccer, and basketball.

RONNIE ROSS, 11

The Isle of Spice

The people as warm as a cup of coffee
Will make your day as sweet as toffee
The food we eat is tasty
Makes you go crazy

The national dish is oil down*
You can find it anywhere in town
We have a variety of fish
So you can make a fabulous dish

The sand is sparkling white
What a wonderful sight
As the wind blows against the sea
It's a lovely view to see

ADREENE FORSYTH, 10

* Dish cooked in coconut milk until all the milk is absorbed, leaving a bit of coconut oil in the bottom of the pan

The Isle of Spice

The people as warm as a cup of coffee
Will make your day as sweet as toffee
The food we eat is tasty
Makes you go crazy

The national dish is oil down
You can find it anywhere in town
We have a variety of fish
So you can make a fabulous dish

The sand is sparkling white
What a wonderful sight
As the wind blows against the sea
It's a lovely view to see

Guatemala | Central America

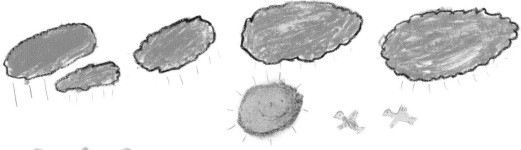

We speak many languages, but mostly Spanish. • We eat tortillas, black beans, rice, and fried bananas. • We play soccer, basketball, and volleyball.

Thank you Guatemala
For giving life to our grandparents.
Thank you for the roads.
Thank you for the food.
For giving us a school where we can study
And learn a lot of things.
Welcome to those who visit us.
Thank you for the dinner that we eat.
Thank you Guatemala.

ANA TUM LOPEZ, 13

Maltiox oximolew xakiitzaj qamam
maltiox oxom qabe xaquje oxom qawa
maltiox oxom qabix xaquje oxom tijobal
maltiox chawe utz pitik uchanim koquk'
maltioxij chiwe qajanik tzijo uchanim
xaquje atom qasi xaquje illom ga
xaquje illom tinamit kot maltiox oxom che

CATARINA LUX US, 11

148

Guinea | Africa

We speak many languages, but our official language is French.   •   We eat rice with meat, squash, and fruit.   •   We play soccer and basketball.

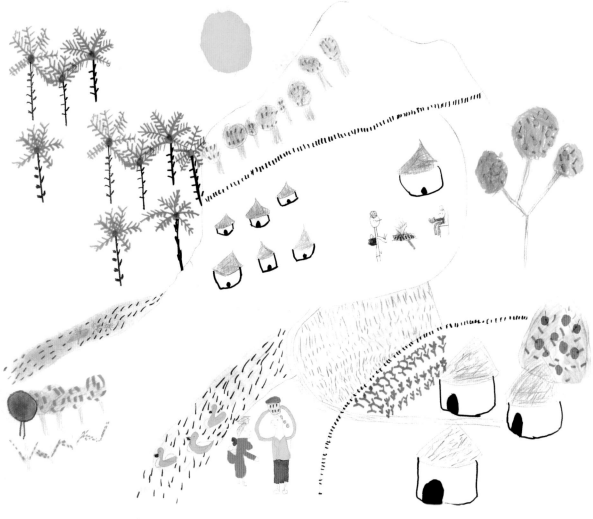

STUDENTS OF ECOLE SAINTE MARIE, 10

My Beautiful Village

Blessed land of my grandparents
My village is dressed in a natural boubou*
Made of vegetation, mountains, and flows of water
Long and numerous rains through the year
Make my village and its surroundings, the source of life
The inexhaustible granary of the country
Enlightened by the shining rising sun
Illuminated by the sweetness of the moon and the stars
My village is a gift of God
Paradise of the good-hearted, I love you.

MAHAWA CONDE, 10

* Large African dress usually very colorful, worn by men and women

Mon beau village.
-Terre bénie de mes grands-parents
Mon village est habillé d'un boubou naturel
-Fait de végétation, de reliefs et de cours d'eau
-Des pluies nombreuses et longues au cours
de l'année
-Font de mon village et les environs la source
de vie
-Le grenier inépuisable du pays
-Eclairé par les éclats du soleil levant
-Illuminé par la douceur de la lune et des
étoiles.
-Mon village est un don de Dieu
-Paradis des bienheureux, je t'aime!

Guinea Bissau | Africa

We speak Kriolu, but our official language is Portuguese. • We eat mostly rice dishes, along with fish or meat, and tropical fruits. • We play soccer.

Guinea Bissau
A small country
Quiet, but with
Destructions from the war.

Guinea Bissau
HIV still there
People still rising to die.

Guinea Bissau
A country with cholera
But thanks to health campaigns
It will improve.

Guinea Bissau
A country with many small islands
Is already on the way to reconciliation
With the people.

Guinea Bissau
A nice country
With many flavorful
Fruits and beaches.

TIAGO COSTA, 10

JOANA DJALO RIBEIRO SANTIAGO, 10

Guiné Bissau
Um País Pequeno
e calmo com
destruiçãos de guerra

Guiné Bissau
Ainda com vírus
de sida muitas
Pessoas ainda em risco de falecer

Guiné Bissau
um País com cólera
que com as campanhas
ão a melhorar

Guiné Bissau
Um País com várias Ilhotas
e justa em reconciliação
com o Povo

Guiné Bissau
Um País bonito
e com frutos
com o Povo com Praias

Guyana | South America

We speak English. • We eat rice, seafood, spicy curry, meat pies, and *roti* (unleavened bread). • We play cricket, soccer, field hockey, tennis, and golf.

DIANNA AND SOFROH HOSEA, 9

Guyana is my homeland
A beautiful place
We work hand in hand
With smiles on our faces

Batavia is my community
We live as one in unity
It's full of friendly people

It's found in the Cuyuni River
Near to the Kamaria Range
With fifty-two falls*
It's like heaven to all

HELENA LYTE AND RAY MCWATT, 9

* Multiple rapid waterfalls in the Cuyuni

Guyana is my home land
A Beautiful place
We work hand in hand
With smiles on our faces

Batavia is my community
We live as one in unity
It's full of friendly people

It's found in the cuyuni River
Near to the Kamaria Range
With fitty two falls
It's like heaven to all

Haiti | Central America

We speak Haitian Creole and French. • We eat rice and beans every day, as well as seafood, fruit, and meat-filled pastries. • We play soccer.

JONAS MARCELUS, 11

Haiti marvelous country!
Haiti the sunny country!
I want to claim your beauty
To all those who have forgotten you.

I shall always return to your feet
Even when I go very far away
To come and praise
The sweetness of your plains.

Dear Haiti I love you
Your fresh mountains
Sweetening our nights
Ayiti Toma* is a very dear country.

Haiti I love you
It's in your arms that I want to die!

PIERRE BRÉCHEL CHÉRY, 10

* Creole name of Haiti in which
Ayiti is the first name and Toma
the last name of the country

Ayiti peyi mèvèy!
Ayiti peyi solèy!
Mwen vle fè konnen bèlte-w
A tout sila-yo ki bliye-w.

m-ap toujou retounen
menm lè-m pati byen lwen
pou-m vinn ba-w ochan
nan mitan bonjan van.

Ayiti cheri mwen renmen-w anpil
Gen bon ti van
Ki ban nou bon ti frechè
Ayiti Toma se yon peyi ki mè chè

Ayiti mwen renmen-w anpil anpil
Se nan bra-w pou mwen mouri!

Honduras | Central America

PATRICK MIGUEL M., 11

Honduras

I

A mi me gusta mi país
mi país Honduras
Por las maravillas que hay en sus campos
que me llenan de dulsura.

II

Cuando paseo por las calles
las calles de San Pedro
Veo a unos Jovenes
que platican de ello.

III

Cuando Juego en el campo
Observo una Flor,
Pruebo una Fruta
¡que rico Sabor!

IV

Cuando voy a las islas de la bahía
voy a buscar,
viendo los hermosos tesoros
que hay en el mar.

VI

A mi me gusta mi país
mi país Honduras
Por las maravillas que hay en sus camp
que me llenan de dulsura

Honduras

I like my country
My country Honduras
For the wonders of its fields
Filling me with sweetness.

Whenever I walk its streets
The streets of San Pedro*
I see young people
Chatting about all this.

Whenever I play in the fields
I look at a flower,
I taste fruits
What a flavor!

Whenever I visit the Islas de la Bahía**
I go diving,
And look at the beautiful treasures
In the sea.

I like my country
My country Honduras
For the wonders of its fields
Filling me with sweetness.

KARLA PATRICIA, 11

* San Pedro Sula is the second-largest city in Honduras
** Bay Islands is one of the eighteen departments in
which Honduras is divided

158

Hungary | Europe

We speak Hungarian. • We eat *gulyás* (goulash), dumplings, potatoes, *halászlé* (fish soup), and stuffed peppers. • We play soccer and tennis.

When I think of my country:
I think of the shops, the traffic,
The beautiful roads, and all the cars.
I think of the combino car*
Because it looks great
And the chain bridge**
Because there are two lions on it.
I think of the well-being of my family
The love of my friends
My little rabbit
I think that I am alive
That we have something to eat and to drink
And that we can pay the school.

HANNAH, ANNA, ALEX, 9

* Low floor tramway
** A suspension bridge spanning the
River Danube between Buda and Pest

Ez jut eszembe az országomról
 et boltgk a forgalmas utak
es a mellék utak gyönyörüek és sok
jármü van
galambos Hannah oldalka
Combino mert szép.
Lánchid mert az elején van
két oroszlán.

A családom épsége:
A barátnőim szeretete.
A kis nyuszim.
Az hogy élek. Az hogy van
mit ennünk, innnunk. Az
hogy tugyuk fizetni a
lakhelő iskolát.

ANDRÁSI SZILVIA, 9

160

Iceland | Europe

We speak Icelandic. • We eat fish, lamb, potatoes, and *hangikjöt* (smoked mutton). • We play soccer, basketball, handball, and golf.

INGI GUDMUNDSSON, 12

Iceland

Iceland is small
But still so big
We are in the middle of the ocean
And a part of the world
We have volcanoes
We have glaciers
We have rivers
We have lakes
We have lava
We have waterfalls
All in one island
I feel like I know everyone in Iceland
And that everyone knows me
Then I watch the news
And I find out . . .
That I know so few

PORDIS OLOF SIGURJONSDOTTIR, 12

India | Asia

We speak many languages, but mostly Hindi. • We eat a variety of very spicy rice dishes and curries. • We play cricket, soccer, and hockey.

SAMMAT MANJU HANSA, 13

Water Comes

Mmmmmh the water comes
Mmmmmh the water comes
On houses, on markets
On trees, on fields

Mmmmmh the water comes
Slish-slosh the water comes
Cold cold water comes
Pleasing everyone's body and mind

Children started dancing in it
Even I started jumping in it
Mmmmmh the water comes
Mmmmmh the water comes

SHINIKA AND BALIKAY, 13

पानी आमा
अर र र पानी आमा।
हर र र पानी आमा॥
घरो पर बाजारो पर।
पेड़ो पर मैदानो पर।

अर र र पानी आमा
रिम – झिम – रिम झिम पानी आमा॥
ठण्डा- ठण्डा पानी आमा॥
सबके तन मन को आमा॥

बच्चे करो नाचने उसमे
मैं भी लगी कूद नेउसमे
अर र र पानी आमा
हर र र पानी आमा

164

Indonesia | Asia

We speak Indonesian. • We eat rice, coconut milk, seafood, and *sop bening* (vegetable soup). • We play soccer, basketball, volleyball, and tennis.

RIZKA M., 10

The Greengrocer

Since dawn, your wheels are already in movement
From one place to another
To meet families' needs
Vegetables . . . vegetables! And many ladies come out
To buy vegetables
The greengrocer is happy
Because all the vegetables were sold
The greengrocer and his family
Are kneeling to praise God

DEWI SVIISTIA, 10

Pedagang Sayur

Dari ufuk timur banmu telah menggelinding.
dari wilayah ke wilayah lain.
Untuk membutuhi kebutuhan keluarga.

Sayur --- sayur lalu ibu-ibu datang menghampiri.
Untuk membeli sayuran itu.
Pedagang sayur itu sangat senang.

Karena sayurannya telah habis terjual.
Pedagang sayur itu dan keluarganya.
bersimpuh mengucap syukur.

Iran | Asia (Middle East)

We speak Farsi, Kurdish, Luri, and Arabic. • We eat rice, meat-and-vegetable stew, and yogurt. • We play soccer, basketball, and table tennis.

KIMIA ASSADIAN, 9

« بسم الله الرحمن الرحیم »

تمام افتخار خود را
از سر وطن می دانم

دو وطن خود ایران را
بهترین جمع می دانم

تمام همه مسافران وخوب
کیکیرا خصوبک خانواده ی دانم

از البرز تا زاکرس
همه جا گل و دریا

همه جا سبز و زیبا
دارد برف دریا ایران را

دارد ایران ٤ فصل را
دارد ماه و مهتاب

دارد خورشید آفتاب
همه کیش خوشاب

دوست دارم هم را
دوست دارم هم کیایش

بیشترین ایران
من کشور ایران

بجته مبارک و باهش
کشور باتم کبر دست

جیو دنیا کنت نویسی
کوشت شاعامه ارسال بی

جو ایران باشد نم ماد
من بوم در رکایک من ماد

I am very proud
Because of Iran
There is no place better than Iran my
homeland
Everyone is hospitable and nice
We know each other as one big family

From the Caspian Sea to the Persian Gulf
From Alborz to Zagros mountains
Everywhere is green and beautiful,
Full of forest and lakes
Iran has four seasons:
It has snow and rain

It has sun and sunshine
It has moon and moonlight
It is attractive everywhere
Everyone is cheerful
I love my compatriots
I love every bit of Iran

The children are smart and clever
They're all friends
How nicely Ferdowsy* in his masterpiece
Shahname** wrote:
"If it wasn't for Iran, I wouldn't be alive."

HELIA KAVOOSI, 10

* Very famous eleventh-century Persian poet   ** Very long poem counting the history of Iran

Iraq

Asia (Middle East)

We speak many languages, but our official language is Arabic. • We eat *khubz* (flat bread), rice, vegetable stews, and fruit. • We play soccer.

ALIND SHERZAD, 11

Spring, bride of all seasons
Season of blossoming flowers
Children, youth together,
Go to picnics together, happily
To the forests, plains, mountains
Hold ceremonies and sing songs
With the sounds of warbling birds

AYIA AMIR ISMAEL, 11

يو ماربيكا ه ه مى ورزانه
ورز عت يشقينا گولانه
زارو كوكه نم بينكه دى جنه سيوانا
لخاف دا رسان و دشت وجيايانه
ه هى دگه ل ننك بدله كئ نوش
ناهه نگوسل نادگئز ديزا
دگه ل دهنكئ بلبلال هه ردارا .

Ireland | Europe

We speak Irish and English. • We eat seafood, potatoes, and *crubeens* (pig feet). • We play Gaelic football (combination of soccer and basketball).

CIAN MCLOUGHLIN, 12

Ireland is green,
And clean.

Ireland is nice,
Although it has a high price.

Ireland is small,
That's why we only have like one shopping mall.

Ireland is old,
And very cold.

JACK FARELL, 13

Ireland is green,
and clean.

Ireland is nice,
although it has a high price.

Ireland is small,
that's why we only have like one shopping mall.

Ireland is old,
and very cold.

Israel

Asia (Middle East)

We speak Hebrew, Arabic, Russian, and English. • We eat *falafel* (pita bread with chickpeas) and spicy fish dishes. • We play soccer and basketball.

May God give us rain
So we could bathe without guilt
May peace be in our country
So our dreams come true
And we live in peace of mind and happiness
With lots of love

ORI, 9

STUDENTS OF NETANYA DEMOCRATIC SCHOOL, 9

Italy | Europe

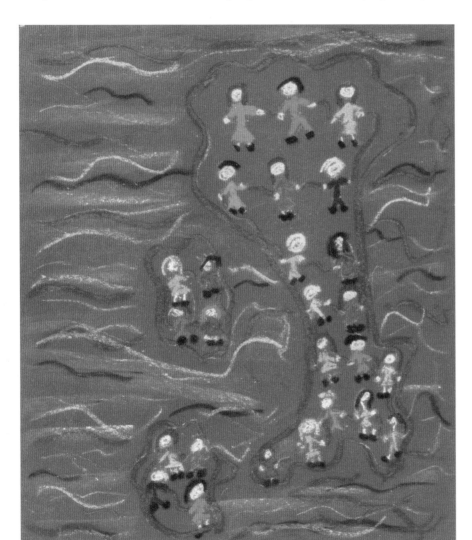

DEBORAH SEBASTIANI, 10

L'Italia è il moi stivale variopinto :
C'è il marrone delle montagne,
Il verde delle pianure,
Il beige delle colline
E l'azzuro del mare,
Rosa, giallo, viola, arancione sono le regioni.
Il bello, però viene dentro lo stivale.
Persone con accenti diversi
Sulle "A" sulle "E" sulle "I" sulle "O"
sulle "U".
Cambiano i vestiti,
Le usanze e i monumenti,
Il colosseo a Roma, il Duomo a Milano.
Il clima delle regioni è diverso,
In alcune fa sempre caldo,
In alcune sempre freddo,
Ma tutte sono belle.
L'Italia è speciale
E per questo non debe cambiare!!

Italy is my multicolored boot:
There is the brown of the mountains,
The green of the meadows,
The beige of the hills,
And the light blue of the sea,
Pink, yellow, purple, orange are the regions.
The beauty comes from the boot:
People with different accents
On the "A," on the "E," on the "I," on the "O,"
and on the "U,"
The different clothing,
The habits, and the monuments,
Rome's Coliseum* and Milano's Duomo**
The weather in the regions are diverse,
Some are always warm,
Others are always cold,
But all of them are beautiful.
Italy is a special country
For that reason it must never change!!

LAURA MASTELOTTO, 10

* Amphitheater in the city center of Rome,
built during the Roman Empire
** Cathedral church

176

Jamaica | Central America

We speak English. • We eat stews and curries, *jerk* (spicy barbecued pork or chicken), and *bammy* (cassava bread). • We play cricket and soccer.

SHIRLEY, 10

I Love Jamaica

I love Jamaica because it is a beautiful country
I love Jamaica because it has wonderful flowers
I love Jamaica because it has lots of music
I love Jamaica because it has wonderful dishes
I love Jamaica because it has a beautiful climate
I love Jamaica because it has beautiful beaches
And I love Jamaica because it is a beautiful place.

SHAQUILLA, 9

Japan | Asia

We speak Japanese. • We eat rice, fresh vegetables, seafood, noodles, soups, and sushi. • We play baseball, soccer, and golf, and we like martial arts.

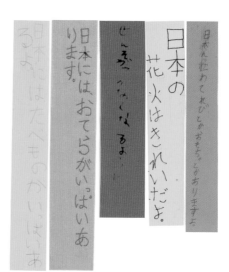

In Japan there are many foods
In Japan there are many temples
I hope there will be no war
Japanese fireworks are beautiful
In Japan there are televisions and toys

MAI, REIRA, YUUKA, RYOTA, 8

日本の花火はきれいだよ。

日本にはおてらがいっぱいあります。

じ〜ぞ〜もいっぱいなるよ。

日本んなめてえびとかおもち、とうあります

WATABE SHUN, 7

Jordan | Asia (Middle East)

We speak Arabic. • We eat *mansaf* (rice with stewed lamb), *mahshi* (stuffed vegetables), and *meshwi* (shish kebab). • We play soccer and volleyball.

Jordan My Hometown

Jordan my precious country
Your hills and meadows are planted with olive trees,
You are the moon among the planets,
The men are strong willed
Your buildings and sites testify about your history
Jerash, Ajloun*, Keral**, and Petra***,
The Dead Sea and the Aqaba coast,
Let us all cry out loud,

      and long live our king Abdullah the second

Oasis of serenity
A symbol of peace
The poets have written the most beautiful songs
And proud just like your mountains
And the many civilizations that lived there
The rose red City
Its wonderful fish, seashells, and corals
God bless Jordan

NAHLA AL-JITTAN, 10

* Cities with important
ancient ruins
** Fortress
*** Archaeological site,
one of the new wonders
of the world

بلدي الأردن

بلدي الأردن يا غالي
بسهولك وهضابك المزروعة
أنت كالقمر بين الكواكب
وجبالك شامخة تعلوا
مهد حضارات وتاريخ
جرش وقلعة عجلون والكرك
والبحر الميت وشط العقبة
فالندعوا جميعا بصوت واحد

أنت واحة من الأمان
بشجر الزيتون رمز السلام
يتغنى بك الشعراء ويكتب فيك أجمل الألحان
ورجالك أشداء أولو العزم لا يرضون بالهوان
تشهد عليها الآثار والمباني
والبتراء وردية الصخر والجنان
بأصدافه وأسماكه الملونة بلون المرجان
عاشت الأردن وعاش الملك عبدالله الثاني

كلنا الأردن وكلنا فداء لهذا الوطن السامي

AHMAD TAYSEER, 12

Kazakhstan | Asia

We speak Kazakh and Russian. • We eat *pierozhki* (meat- or potato-filled pastries), potatoes, and wild berries. • We play soccer and ice hockey.

Native country, you are so near for me
I know all your ways,
I recognize you anywhere!

Azure sky, snowy mountains
Powerful steppes, wild scopes,
Wonderful rivers, bottomless lakes,
Children's joy again and again!

New high buildings, parks, and squares,
Evening walks, green alleys,
Shining sun, thick forests,
Birds singing and don't pity anything!

Aqua-parks, restaurants,
Pizzas, sandwiches, cafe-bars!!!
Cinemas and theatres, laughter anywhere
Because Kazakhstan is the best!!!

HABIROVA MARYAM, 12

FIRSOVA KATAY, 10

Родная страна, ты так близка,
Мне каждая тропинка здесь знакома.
Тебя я узнаю из далека
Ведь лучше места нет, родного дома!

Чистое небо, Снежные горы
Могучие степи, Бескрайние просторы,
Восхитительные реки, Глубокие озёра,
Радость детей снова и снова!

Новейшие здания, парки и скверы,
Вечерние прогулки, зелёные деревья,
Ослепительное солнце, Зелёные аллеи,
Птички поют, Ни о чём не жалея!

Аква - парки, рестораны,
пицца, сендвич, кафе- бары!!!
Кинотеатры, театры, смех
Казахстан ведь лучше всех!!!

Kenya | Africa

We speak English and Kiswahili. • We eat fish, red bean stew, *chapati* (flat bread), and *sukuma wiki* (collard greens). • We play soccer and like running.

PEOPLE IS DANCING   ISukuti

YVONNE KHUSOA, 10

Oh Matatu*

Listen little green matatu
Rushing down the dusty road
Packed with people and luggage
Tell me why you take such loads,
Why? Because I want to help you,
Take you where you want to go,
Take your maize and fruit to markets
That is why I am loaded so
Then listen, little green matatu
Look how many cars you have passed
If you're full of goods and people
Is it safe to overspeed?

AILEEN NECHESA, 10

* Small minibuses used for transportation, known for driving very fast

oh matatu
litsen little green matatu,
rushing down the dusty road
buciset with people Good and laguage,
tell me why you take such loads,
why? beacause i want to help you,
take you where you want to go,
take your maize and fruit to market,
that is why am loaded so,
then litsen little green matatu
look how many cars you have past
if your full of Goods and people
is it safe to overspeed?

Kiribati | Oceania

We speak Kiribati, but our official language is English. • We eat coconuts, fish, breadfruit, papaya, and rice. • We play soccer and volleyball.

Sea

E bongana taarii bwa a Mau iai ika
E kamau tarii irouia ataei bwa aia tabo n tebotebo
E tikiraoi tarii bwa ngaia ae ti Mau iai
E nang kamau tarii iaon Kiribati bwa aitiaki
E bongana tarii bwa te tabo ni mwamwananga
nato buki

CAISILO, 13

Sea

It is useful the sea, because fish live in it
It is fun for kids the sea, as it is a swimming place
It is great, the sea, as it provides for us
It is clean, the sea in Kiribati
It is useful the sea, for journeys to far away islands.

BWETERA, 13

Korea, North (DPRK) | Asia

We speak Korean. • We eat very spicy foods, like *kimch'i* (spicy pickled cabbage), and many rice dishes. • We play soccer, volleyball, and table tennis.

MUN HYOK JIN, 11

《사회주의 나나라》

1련 사회주의 너나라
참좋은 나라
누구나 배우며
일하는 나라

2련 장군님의 령도밑에
우리 인민
하나로 뭉친
일심단결의나라

3련 어디에 가나
볼수 있으리
사람들의
명랑한 모습을

4련 깨끗하고 아름다운
거리와 마을은
또 얼마나
환홀한가

5련 아, 우리나라는
세상에서
으뜸가는
사회주의나라

우리나라에
꼭 와보세요

3중영예 붉은기 평양릉라소학교
3학년 2반 9살 김송

My Socialist Country

My socialist country
How good it is
Where we all study
Where we all work

The single-minded united country
Where everyone
Is united as one
Under the general's leadership

You can see
Wherever you go
The cheerful looks
Of the people

How grand
They are also,
The clean and beautiful
Streets and villages

Oh, our country is
The socialist country,
The best
In the world

KIM SONG, 9

190

Korea, South | Asia

We speak Korean. • We eat very spicy foods, *kimch'i* (spicy pickled cabbage), and rice dishes. • We play baseball and soccer, and we like martial arts.

LEE SEUNG HYUN, 13

We Are the Red Devils!*

When we watched the World Cup game,
I saw a goal
A big piece of paper
Into the small hole
Wow!
The ball that our player kicked
Goal in
Players and spectators
Run in pleasure,
A pleasure as big as the soccer ground

KIM MIN JI, 13

* Official supporting group for South Korea's national soccer team

한국 서울 양서중학교 1학년
14살 김민지 ^^*

우리는 붉은악마

김민지 지음

월드컵보다가
쳐다본 골대
커다란 도화지 한장안
조그만 구멍속으로

아아
우리선수들 찬 공이
쏙 들어간다.

선수들도
관 객들도
뛰어들어가는
축구장만한 기쁨속.

Kuwait | Asia (Middle East)

We speak Arabic and English. • We eat a wide variety of rice dishes and we drink *laban* (a yogurt-based drink). • We play soccer and water sports.

The Smile of Kuwait

We are the smile of Kuwait
We are its tears flowing into quarries
We are a rainbow in its sky
We are the children of Kuwait

We are the flowers of its garden
We are the light of truth
We are the enemies of guns
We refuse to see in our fields the light of fire

Our land Kuwait was and still is
The place of love
We used to live from our sea
And thanks to her we could live in the past
How can we accept to see birds' nests
destroyed in our homeland?

DALAL AL-NAJM, 9

LOLWA ADEL, 7

ابتسامة الكويت

نحن ابتسامة الكويت في الفرح

ونحن دمعها في المحاجر انسفح

ونحن في سمائها قـوس قزح

نحـن أبنـاء الكـويت

نحـن أزهـار الحـديقة

نحـن أنـوار الحـقيقة

نحـن أعـداء البنـادق

نحن نأبى أن نرى في حقلنا وجه الحرائق

أرضنـا الكـويت كـانت وتبـقى

دوحـة الحب الكبيـر

بحـرنا قـد كان رزقـًا

وبـه عشنـا دهـورًا

كيف نرضى في ربانا هدم أعشاش الطيور؟

Kyrgyzstan | Asia

We speak Kyrgyz and Russian. • We eat *beshbarmak* (noodles and meat), rice, and mutton. • We play soccer, basketball, and *ulak* (type of polo).

MOMUN KYZY OROZGUL, 14

Kyrgyzstan

Kyrgyzstan, such a spectacular country,
such a beautiful country
The roaring waters are the most wonderful
Blue rivers are running down and their murmur
is like a song to your ears.

I will live in Kyrgyzstan forever
And will devote my life to Kyrgyzstan,
Spectacular here, and beautiful there,
For the sake of those many beautiful places,
My soul will never rest.

AICHUROK AIJIGITOVA, 14

Кыргызстан.
Кыргызстан кандай кооз,
кандай сулуу.
Шылдыраган суулары
Эң жукумдуу,
Когоргон дарыяса агып
тушкен
Үчүн укаар кулакка
тамшыгуу.
Я
Кыргызстанда жашай мен
мен эрдайым,
Өмурумду бир умуга
арнаймын.
Бул жердин кооз - кооз
жерлерине,
Жанымда да эч убакта
албаймын.

Laos | Asia

We speak French and Lao. • We eat sticky rice, *paa* (spicy fish soup), and stir-fry. • We play soccer, volleyball, and basketball.

MONETHONG, 12

Laos's Nature

Last week, my parents took me and my family to Ban Ken Village.

There, I saw many beautiful trees, they're big and green.

At the same time I saw some animals: birds, mice, squirrels, monkeys.

They ran from tree to tree, it was amazing to see them;

and then a small wind passed by; it made bamboo trees hit each other and the sound was pretty good.

In the morning before the sunrise a fog covers all the sky and makes me feel warm.

Here the nature and animals live together, and they are all happy with each other.

I've said to my parents and my family that if I have a chance I will come here again because I want to learn, and stay close to the nature.

I'm very happy that my parents and my family took me there.

It makes me happy and I got some experiences from the nature and animals.

VELL MANE PHICHID, 14

198

Latvia | Europe

We speak Latvian and Russian. • We eat soup, potatoes, red meat, and fruit and vegetables. • We play soccer, volleyball, and basketball.

VINETA SILINA, 9

I Live in Latvia

I'm Latvian and born in Latvia. I like Latvia very much and I think it's the most beautiful. Latvia is located on the left side of world (I think so) and it has the shape of heart. We have seas, rivers, and lakes. Here vegetate spruces, pine trees, oaks, birch trees, aspen trees, junipers, and other trees and plants. But the most beautiful place in Latvia is Kemeri. There is Kemeri National Park where the nature is very abundant and beautiful. Everybody likes very much the swamp. There you can walk around along footbridges, you can see rare plants, birds, and animals. We often go there for walk because it' s good place to have a rest. Welcome and you will see this all by yourself!

MARTENS RIBAKS, 10

Es dzīvoju Latvijā!

Es esmu latvietis un piedzimu Latvijā.

Man Latvija loti patīk un es domāju ka tiņa ir visskaistākā.

Latvija atrodas Zemes kreisajā pusē (tā es domāju), viņai ir sirds forma. Mums ir jūra, upes un ezeri. Latvijā aug egles, priedes, ozoli, bērzi, apses, kadiķi un vēl daudz augi.

Bet visskaistākā vieta Latvijā ir Kemeri. Tod ir Kemeru nacionālais parks. Daba ir loti bagāta un skaista. No zemes nāk sērūdeņi, kuri ir loti veselīgi. Visiem loti patīk purvs.

Tur var staigāt pa vētraisitām laipām, var redzēt daudz retus augus, putnus, dzīvniekus. Mēs biezi ejam staigāt pa laipāmi, tur loti atpūsties. Brauciet pie mums ciemos, un visu pati redzēsiet!!!

Lebanon

Asia (Middle East)

We speak Arabic and French. • We eat various meat stews and some vegetarian dishes. • We play soccer, but we also like skiing and swimming.

The Lebanese Taxi Driver

He earns money driving
He drives smiling
He often shouts at other cars
He always stops all at once
He transports bigger ones and smaller ones
Shouting, he passes the red light
He waits hours for a client to come
He is a nice and funny man

MALEK KAEDKEY, 10

MYRIAM ALI AHMAD AND LINE ITANI, 10

Le chauffeur de taxi Libanais

Il prend l'argent en conduisant

Il conduit la voiture en souriant

Il crie après les voitures souvent

Il arrête toujours brusquement

Il transporte les petits et les grands

Il traverse le feu rouge en criant

Il attend des heures un client

C'est un homme gentil et est amusant

Lesotho | Africa

We speak English and Sesotho. • We eat rice, potatoes, fruit and vegetables, and *papa* (stiff cornmeal porridge). • We play soccer and volleyball.

TEBOHO LEKHOTI, 12

Temo Lesotho

Lona batho ba Lefatse lohle
Greng ke le bolelle
Re lula Lesotho
M'e re Basotho

Re seketsa ka thata
Re phela ka ho itemela masimo
ke kamoo Molimo are bopileng

Re tsoha esale ka meso
Re leme masimo, re hlaole le ho kotula
Re ja litsoa-mobung
le meroho ho tsoa lirapeng

Bathusi ba rona ke phoofolo tsa rona
Maloting ho lengoa koro, kerekesi le lentšil
Mabalane Poone, linaoa le mabele

Plowing in Lesotho

People from all over the world
Let me tell you this
We live in Lesotho
And we are Basotho

We are hard-working people
We do not have to buy everything
We live by plowing our fields
That is how God made us

We rise up early in the morning
Plow our fields, hoe or reap our crops
We eat crops from our fields
And vegetables from our gardens

Our helpers are animals we rear
In the highlands wheat, peas, and lentils are planted
In the lowlands maize, beans,
And sorghum are planted

LIENGOANE MALEFANE, 11

Liberia | Africa

We speak many languages, but mostly English. • We eat rice dishes, okra, fish and other seafood, and goat. • We play soccer, basketball, and kickball.

EDWARD BLACKIE, 17

Oh! How happy I am
To see my country with stable peace
To see everyone moving so happy
To hear that Mother Liberia is back

Oh! How happy I am
To believe that a president is elected
To hear that development is back to
Mama Liberia
To see the youth of Mama Liberia looking happy

Oh! How happy I am
To see various countries helping Mama Liberia
To see little children playing and laughing
To see all tribes of Mama Liberia
working together in unity

Oh! How happy I am
To congratulate all those who give Mama Liberia
peace
To thank all those who risk their life for
Mama Liberia
To console those feelings that were hurt

Oh! How happy I am
To thank the almighty God for hearing the holy
prayers
To believe that we are saved once more

Oh! How happy I am
For development
For peace and stability
Long live Mama Liberia

AMUNEE WHEREMONGER, 18

Libya | Africa

We speak Arabic. • We eat *sharba libiya* (Libyan soup), pasta dishes, and fruit and vegetables. • We play soccer, volleyball, and basketball.

So much sand!
So much sand!
"This is really detestable"
Vociferates a dromedary
Very peaky on dust
It will take me the whole life
To sweep the desert!

MAHMOUD MAJBLAR, 10

Que de sable !
Que de sable !
C'est vraiment détestable
réocifère un dromadaire
Très à cheval sur la poussière
Il me faudra la ville entière
Cour balayer le désert !

LEILA BUZRIGH, 10

208

Liechtenstein | Europe

We speak German. • We eat sandwiches, soup, salad, and *rösti* (fried grated potatoes). • We play soccer, but we also like gymnastics and cycling.

NADINE KOLBENER, 12

Liechtenstein

Liechtenstein has fields
Banks have loads of money
We have the best school
All the guests like it!
It has many mountains
But unfortunately no dwarfs
Parents scold
And grandparents skate.
It doesn't have sea
But we have much tar.
In the houses live many clerks
I really like Liechtenstein
But I also like to live by the sea!

LAURA DE ICCO, 13

Liechtenstein

In Liechtenstein hats Fei
auf den Banken liegen viele ...
Unsere Schule ist die beste
beliebt bei allen gäste'.
Es hat viele berge
aber leider keine Zwerge.
Die Eltern schelten
und die Grosseltern skatern.
Es hat kein meer
aber dafür sehr viel Teer.
In den Häusern
leben viele Verkäufern.
In Liechtenstein gefällts mir sehr
aber ich wohne auch gerne am Meer!!!

Lithuania | Europe

We speak Lithuanian. • We eat *blynai* (pancakes), *barščiai* (beet soup), and smoked sausages. • We play basketball, soccer, volleyball, and tennis.

ANTANO VIENUDIO, 11

Motherland

A birch is weeping at the foot of a hill,
There's a castle way up there.
Here is the fatherland most precious
Here we all grew and grew.

It's beautiful when you look around
All green in the world and your heart
It's so nice to live under the sun,
It's so good to have a home.

I'd like to make my land famous
A land told about in many songs
For its firm will and courage
For freedom, for language, for truth …

VIKTORIJA JILOBRIT, 11

Tėvynė

Pakalnėj linguoja berželis,
Ant kalno stovi pilis.
Čia protėvių žemė brangiausia,
Čia augom ir augom visi.

Gražu apsidairius aplinkui –
Vien žalia aplink ir širdy.
Taip miela gyventi po saule,
Taip gera turėti namus.

Norėčiau aš garsinti šalį,
Ne kart apdainuotą dainoj,
Už tvirtą jos valią ir drąsą,
Už laisvę, už kalbą, už tiesą …

Luxembourg | Europe

We speak Luxembourgish, French, and German. • We eat *Bouneschlupp* (bean soup), sausages, potatoes, and sauerkraut. • We play soccer.

JOSHUA DEFAYS AND SARAH SCHMITZ, 10

LUXEMBURG/LETZEBUERG

Mir liewen an engem friddlecche hand.
Wou oft Wand bleist.

An eisem hand bleist och vill Loft.

An an dem hand huet jiddereen en Haus.
Am Haus leeft villeicht eng Maus

Baueren gët et genuch.
A Bësdie dier gët et vill,
sech ech mengen iwer zing.

Op de Spillplazen gët et Schaukelen un, dëi machen wing wing

Zu Veranen gët et eng Buerg.
Dat Land van deem ech lo schwëtzen,
heitt Lëtzebuerg.

Luxembourg / Letzebuerg*

We are leaving in a peaceful country
Where the wind often blows
In our country also blows a lot of love
And in this country, everyone has a house
In that house might live a mouse

There are enough farmers
And many forests
More than ten I believe

On the playgrounds there are swings
Singing wing, wing
In Vianden there is a fortress
The country I am telling you about
Is called Luxembourg

JOSHUA DEFAYS, 10

* "Luxembourg" in Luxembourgish

214

Macedonia (FYROM) | Europe

We speak Macedonian and Albanian. • We eat roasted meats, stuffed peppers, and *turshija* (pickled vegetables). • We play basketball and soccer.

ALEXANDER BOGOEVSKI, 11

A stone here, a flower there,
Swallows flying
In the vast blue sky,
The sun is shining everywhere.

The wind blows
A song acknowledging
The booklet babbling
The child singing.

High mountains proudly stretching
Lakes from ancient times
Homeland you are mine
In the Balkans* like a pearl you shine.

ZORAN BOSHKOV, 10

* Geographic region of southern Europe

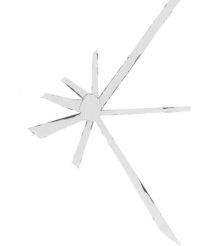

Madagascar | Africa

We speak Malagasy and French. • We eat rice at most meals, fruit, and *romazava* (beef and leaves stew). • We play soccer and like cockfighting.

SOA AIME TAFITA RAZAFINDRAVOLA, 11

Ry Madagasikara

O ry Madagasikara masina
Ianao nosy kely eo antsinanan'i Afrika
Midika zany fa ranomasina no manodidina anao
Tiako ianao, tsy foiko ary tany tsy ho ariko
Fa ianao kanto dia kanto tokoa

Madagasikara ô ! Ianao manana ny maha izy anao
Tsy mitovy amin ireo firenena hafa eto ambonin ny tany
Ianao dia tsy lehibe fahatany fa miraki-java-tsoa
Tia fiharanana sy mivavaka hatrany.

Ny razanay Malagasy dia teto aminao
Raha tsy misy anao zahay Malagasy dia ho lao
Ianao moa taloha dia natao hoe Nosy maitso
Izao moa @ hadalanay dia lasa Nosy mena enao

Zahay manimba anao isanandro, tsy miraharaha anao
Sy manimba ny tarehinao, sy ny voa afafinao

Koa mifona, sy mivalo fa hanarina anao !!
Zaho moa de tsy mahafoy anao.

O ry Madagasikara, azafady amin ny ratsy nataonay anao
Ny zavatra iriko moa de mba hijanona daholo zany rehetra zany
Satria ianao lay Nosy manja ka ho tiako hatrany.

Mahatsiaro sambatra aho ary koa mirary soa

Oh Madagascar

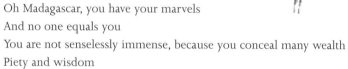

Oh Madagascar the holy
Big island next to Africa
The sea surrounds you
I love you, adore you, and will never deny you
Because you are so wonderful

Oh Madagascar, you have your marvels
And no one equals you
You are not senselessly immense, because you conceal many wealth
Piety and wisdom

Our ancestors have walked on your soil
We exist only by you
There were times when we called you the green island
Nowadays our unconsciousness made us call you the red island

We attack you everyday, and disrespect you
We disfigure you, without any regards

So please forgive us because we will remedy
I myself, will never give you up

Oh Madagascar sorry for all the pain we have caused you
My deepest wish is for that to cease
Because you are this beautiful island I will love forever

Where I feel happy, and I give you all my love

MICHAEL PARFAIT ANDRIANJAKA, 12

Malawi | Africa

We speak Chichewa, Chitumbuka, and English. • We eat dried or fresh fish, goat, red beans, and sugarcane. • We play netball and soccer.

DALITSO PHRI, 14

Malawi what a beautiful country
Malawi the land of lake
A lake with blue waters
What a beautiful lake is this?

A lake with beautiful fish
A lake with hills inside
A lake with beautiful sand
What a beautiful lake is this?

ROSEMIN DAUD, 14

220

Malaysia | Asia

We speak Malay, English, Hindi, and Chinese. • We eat *nasi lemak* (rice steamed with coconut and chlii paste). • We play badminton and soccer.

LIM SOOK TENG, 10

My Country, Malaysia

Malaysia is a country that is beautiful
Everybody there is very peaceful.
Many historical places,
Tourists will enjoy visiting the places.

Food in Malaysia is very delicious,
Some food is nutritious.
Satay, nasi lemak, curry noodles, and curry fishes,
These are the most popular dishes.

Once you come, you will feel safe,
The beaches in Malaysia always have big waves.
A paradise for tourists to stay.
Hotels are cheaper to pay.

Many of Malaysia's children are kind,
They always help those people, such as the blind.
Technologies are growing everyday,
Many people are happy to stay.

SHI YING, 9

Maldives | Asia

We speak Dhivehi and English. • We eat rice and *roshi* (flat bread), and chew betel nuts. • We play soccer and *bashi* (softball with tennis rackets).

MARIYAM NABA NIZAM, 11

Fishes of the Sea

Little fishes in the sea
Why don't you come to me
I love to see you
In the great big sea
I won't harm you
Whether or not you come to me
I just want to see you
In the beautiful sea

Will you come to me ever
So that I can see you
The birds won't eat you
They neither will harm you
So please come to me
In the beautiful sea.

ALYA ALI RASHEED, 10

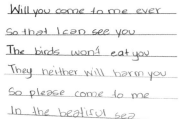

Fishes of the sea
Little fishes in the sea
Why don't you come to me
I love to see you
In the great big sea
I won't harm you
If you come to me or not
I just wont to see you
In the beautiful sea

Will you come to me ever
So that I can see you
The birds won't eat you
They neither will harm you
So please come to me
In the beatiful sea

Mali | Africa

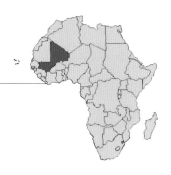

We speak many languages, but mostly French and Bambara. • We eat corn, rice, fresh mangoes, and peanut butter. • We play soccer.

STUDENTS OF BANANKORO FUNDAMENTAL SCHOOL, 9

There is a river in Banankoro
There is bitumen in Banankoro
There is a military camp in Banankoro
There is a school in Banankoro
There is a market in Banankoro
There is mango in Banankoro
There is food in Banankoro
There is solidarity in Banankoro
Oh Banankoro, be our hope.

MOULAYE FAROTA, 10

Poyi Banankoro
Baji be banankoro
Siriba be banankoro
Kan be Banankoro
Kalanso be Banankoro
Sugu Be banankoro
Mangoro be Banankoro
Balobe Banankoro
Hini be Banankoro
Benni ke ma be banankoro.
Banankoro ala ki to a ne sigiye

Malta | Europe

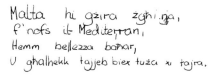

We speak Maltese and English. • We eat *fenkata* (stewed rabbit), *timpana* (macaroni), and *aljotta* (fish chowder). • We play water polo and soccer.

SONJA ALTZINGER, 11

Malta hi gzira zghirja,
f'nofs it-Mediterran,
Hemm bellezza bahar,
U ghalhekk tajjeb biex tuza xi tajra.

Malta hi vera sabiha,
Ghax dejjem hemm is-shana,
U meta tmur xi passiġata,
bil-fors tara xi maltin bhalna,

Il-Fenkata hija ikel tradizzjonali,
U kulhadd jhobb jikolha bhali

F'Malta hemm hafna natura
Kif ukoll hafna kultura

Hemm hafna gzejjer fid-dinja
Imma wahda bhal Malta qatt ha tara

Malta is a small island
In the middle of the Mediterranean Sea
There is a wonderful sea
And you can also play with a kite

Malta is very beautiful
Since it is always hot and sunny
And when you go for a walk
You will for sure see other Maltese

Rabbit stew is the traditional meal
And like me, everybody enjoys eating it

In Malta one can see nature
As well as culture

There are several islands in the world
But Malta is unique

LUKE AAROH AND LUCAS BORG, 10

Marshall Islands | Oceania

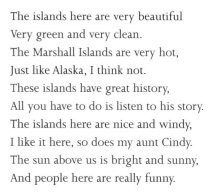

We speak English and Marshallese. • We eat fried or barbecued chicken, fruit, and we drink *ni* (coconut water). • We play basketball and baseball.

The islands here are very beautiful
Very green and very clean.
The Marshall Islands are very hot,
Just like Alaska, I think not.
These islands have great history,
All you have to do is listen to his story.
The islands here are nice and windy,
I like it here, so does my aunt Cindy.
The sun above us is bright and sunny,
And people here are really funny.

JULIE AN RITOK, 12

The Islands here are very beautiful
Very green and very clean.
The Marshall Islands are very hot,
Just like Alaska, I think not.
These Islands have great history,
All you have to do is listen to his story.
The Islands here are nice and windy,
I like it here so does my aunt Cindy.
The sun above us is bright & sunny,
And people here are really funny. •

RANDON JACK, 10

Mauritania | Africa

We speak many languages, but mostly Hassaniya. • We eat rice or couscous every day and drink baobab juice. • We play soccer and like camel racing.

STUDENTS OF ABI HOURAIRA SCHOOL, 10

"Shankit,"* the ideal land,
I've raised my head saying poems
My country; you're my country
My love to my country is a duty to me
For everyone, there is a land
I never get bored from my country

My country is the best
Oh my country, with beautiful expressions
I have known you through time and space
It reinforces my faith
As for forests, there are gazelles
From my life in it; I live two centuries

The Land "Shankit"

* Ancient name for Mauritania

MUSTAFA BOCHRA, 15

لنعم الإوطان شنقيط
رفعت رأس بالشعرقائلا
موطني أنت موطني
حبى لوطني علي واجب
ولكل موأمن موطن
لا أمل يوماس موطني

بلادي هي اغفل الأوطاد
على موطني أحلى المعانها
عرفت في الزمان والمكان
فهذا يزيد من اليمانى
كما للعريش غزلانها
حبد الوفيح أعيش فرنان

الوطن شنقيط

232

Mauritius | Africa

We speak many languages, but mostly French, Hindi, and English. • We eat rice, *roti* (Indian flat bread), and fish. • We play soccer and water sports.

DIERTO BOULAYE, 14

In Mauritius there are many Mauritians
Mauritians are all different and all alike
My name is Laurent
And I am a young boy
Who likes fishing big fish
My friend Sylvain
Likes listening to music
He dances sega and raga
My friend David
Likes to go to discos
In Grand Baie
And my friend Cedric
Likes playing football
On the squares or on the plains
Mauritians are all different and all alike

LAURENT LAVENTURE, 15

a lile maurice Ilya beaucoup de mauricien
les mauriciens Sont Tous different et Tous les memes
moi je mapelle laurent et je suis un petit garçon
qui aime peche les gros poisson mon amis sylvano
Il aime lamusicque, Vle séga et le Raga
Nom Ami DaviD Aime Danser en Discoteque A Grand Baie
et puis Mon Ami CeDric Aime jouer Au football sur
La place ou Dans les pleines les mauriciens Sont tous
different et tous les memes

Mexico | North America

We speak Spanish. • We eat rice, tacos, and *quesadillas* (tortillas with cheese). • We play soccer and baseball, and we like bullfighting.

RICARDO DANIEL PINTO MENDOZA , 15

A Mexican Feeling

The daylight illuminates the path you need to follow
You can feel the waves hugging you
They show you another world.
Wet golden sand,
Shows all your achievements
The reddish sky makes you
Feel the passion
Of a big love.
You feel it,
You see it,
In the Mexican sea.

MARÍA MAGDALENA VARGAS, 12

Sentimiento Mexicano
La luz del sol ilumina el camino que debes seguir,
tú puedes sentir que las olas del mar te abrazan,
y te enseñan otro mundo.
La húmeda arena de oro,
te muestra todos tus logros
el cielo rojizo, te hace
sentir la pasión,
de un gran amor,
todo esto lo sientes,
lo ves,
en el mar mexicano.

Micronesia | Oceania

We speak many languages, but our official language is English. • We eat rice, chicken, and coconuts. • We play basketball and volleyball.

NAIDAN BRADY PERMAN, 15

MY COUNTRY

The Island of Pohnpei is beautiful,
And the people are wonderful
It is clean
With plenty greens.

The weather is Torrid.
At night it is Frigid.
It is really hot
But some people say its not.

From drinking sakau people become lazy
And some became crazy
They walk slowly
And talk softly

The student of CCA
Is deferent from the student of STA
CCA listen to Christian music
While the STA students listen to rock music.

My pastor is Nob Kalau
He never drink sakau.
The people are Kind
But when he starts to talk some always whine.

Anthon Desarach work in a gorement
Where he makes judgement
He is a chief
He loves to carry white handkerchief.

My Country

The island of Pohnpei is beautiful
And the people are wonderful
It is clean
With plenty green.

The weather is torrid
At night it is frigid
It is really hot
But some people say it's not.

From drinking sakau* people become lazy
And some become crazy
They walk slowly
And talk softly.

The students of CCA**
Are different from the students of STA**
CCA listen to Christian music
While the STA students listen to rock music.

My pastor is Nob Kalou
He never drinks sakau
The people are kind
But when he starts to talk some always whine.

Anthon Desarach works in a government
Where he makes judgment
He is a chief
He loves to carry white handkerchief.

KARLA CAPELLE, 10

* Drink with relaxing effects, made from
the roots of a plant for special ceremonies
** Local primary schools

Moldova | Europe

We speak Moldovan and Russian. • We eat *borscht* (tomato and beet soup) and *mititei* (grilled meat sausages). • We play soccer and basketball.

BALAN ANASTASIA, 10

My Country

From Cahul* to Lipcani*
On the road to Buiucani*
You have to walk a long time,
No matter how difficult it can be.
And on your way
Even in the evening
You can see my beautiful country.
With forests and fortresses,
Nice fields,
Famous gardens,
Moldovan people
Proud, strong, and keen.

CRISTINA SOCOLIUC, 10

* Cities in Moldova

Țara mea
De la Cahul pîn la Lipcani
Pe marginea drumului Buiucani
Sunt kilometri mulți de parcurs,
Cît drumul n-ar fi de îngust.
Însă, cît vei mergea
Chiar cînd amurgea
Tot vei vedea superbă țara mea

Păduri și cetățioare au amintiri
Pe veci
Ogoare frumoase,
Grădini faimoase,
Moldoveni gospodari
Mîndri, isteți si tari.

Monaco | Europe

We speak Italian and English, but our official language is French. • We eat olives, vegetables, fish, pizza, and pasta. • We play soccer and tennis.

How beautiful Monaco looks
With its monuments
Controlling the time
And making us dream.
And there is also the museum
And the palace
Which was taken By François Grimaldi*

And the Grand Prix
Avoid it at all costs
If you don't want to become
Tuesday's flat pancake
Eaten by Jake.

And when the cannon fires, don't jump on your feet
If you want to avoid
A cannonball
Shot by my Uncle Paul.

STÉPHANE, 9

* Military officer who took the Rock of Monaco in the thirteenth century

ARNAUD, 9

242

Mongolia | Asia

We speak Mongol. • We eat beef, goat, camel, rice, and *guriltai shul* (mutton-and-noodle soup). • We play yak polo and like wrestling and archery.

ENKHBAYAR KHALIUN, 9

My Motherland

Cloudless blue skies stretch overhead;
Indigo blue mountains are skyscrapers;
This is my country,
Where people live peacefully,
Where animals spread plentifully.
We have
Famous sumo* wrestlers
And world-recognized Olympic champions.
This is the best country on the planet
With millions of the cutest children.

S. BAYASGALAN, 9

* Japanese martial art

We speak many languages, but mostly Montenegrin and Albanian. • We eat seafood and *musaka* (ground beef with potatoes). • We play soccer.

Montenegro in My Heart

Your mountains have been talking for centuries

Clean rivers shine and travel

The sun washes in the waves and stops there,
He wants to stay there forever

My country gave me lots of stars,
I made a birds' nest with them

I love my country like my parents
And I comment on its beauty with my brother

My country is hugging me and kissing me,
I care for her with all my heart!

NIKOLA MARKUS, 10

STELA BOBOT, 10

Morocco | Africa

We speak Arabic and French. • We eat mutton, beef, chicken, and couscous, and we drink mint tea. • We play soccer, volleyball, tennis, and basketball.

Morocco is beautiful	Islam and religion
We have fruits	A beautiful nature
Delicious food	Renown Jelaba*
The color of the sun is red	Snow-capped mountains in winter
Delicious oranges	Long and large dresses

We all love our country Morocco.

*Moroccan dress, used by both women and men   HODA EL KASBAOUI, 12

MIMOUH TAHER, 12

مغربنا جميل « إسلام ودين

فيه ثمار « منظره زايع

طبخ لذيذ « جلبابه معروف

لون شمسه أحمر « قطف شتاء يكسوا

بالجبال « تثمره لذيذ

تلبس ثياسة طويل وعريض

والأمطار

وكلنا نحب بلادنا

مغربنا

Mozambique | Africa

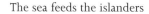

We speak Portuguese. • We eat rice, vegetables, peanuts, and seafood. • We play soccer, basketball, handball, and volleyball.

AMAND SILVERIO, 9, AND MATEUS CARLOS, 13

The sea feeds the islanders
In Mozambique Island there are many historical monuments:
A museum, a hospital, a fortress, a fort, and a bridge
These old buildings are the very history of Ilha de Mozambique*
Women go home after their work
And get ready for the return of their man returning from the sea
They put Musiro** on their faces and gold on their ears and noses
Beautiful, wonderful, and faithful women

QUINTEIRA AMELIA JAMINE, 12

* A small island on the northern coast of Mozambique
** Facial beauty mask used by women made of grated tree bark

O mar é a sobrivivencia das populações
da ILHA a ilha de Mozambique existem varias
especies estoricas como: O Museu, Hopital, a fortaleza, o fortim
a ponte estas coisas velhas é a propria estoria da
Ilha de Mozambiqe.
As mulheres da ilha elas vão para casa depois do
trabalho e sse preparam para o Homem da vinda do
mar vão sse por mussiro e faz maciar a cara poem
ouro na orelha e no nariz mulheres lindas
maravilhosas gostosa de boa fé.
fim: obrigada: Quitiria.

250

Myanmar | Asia

We speak many languages, but our official language is Burmese. • We eat rice, *hin* (curry dish), fried vegetables, and soup. • We play soccer.

CHILDREN FROM THE MYANMAR BUDDHIST ORPHANAGE ASSOCIATION, 10

About Myself and Myanmar

My name is Aie Naut.

I have two elder brothers and two younger sisters.

My grandmother died when I was young.

My mother is a housekeeper

And my father is a farmer.

I used to visit the pagodas* with my uncle and my grandmother.

Phayagyi**, Mandalay Hills***, and Aung Daw Mu Pagoda are famous in Mandalay.

There are so many bicycles

And a few motorcycles and motored cars.

There are also many resorts and spas

And airports and bus terminals.

Myanmar is always green

With paddy fields.

Rainy season is the best in Myanmar.

There are seven states and seven divisions in Myanmar.

Our capital is Yangon****

And there are many famous pagodas there.

Movie stars live in Yangon.

Myanmar has many bridges.

Besides minerals, we produce a lot of oil and coal.

China, Malaysia, Thailand, Laos, India, Singapore, and Vietnam

Are at our surrounding.

CHILDREN FROM THE MYANMAR BUDDHIST ORPHANAGE ASSOCIATION, 11

* Buddhist religious monument
** A monastery in the city of Mandalay
*** Hill located to the northeast of the city center of Mandalay, 240 meters tall
**** Ex-capital city of Myanmar

Namibia | Africa

We speak many languages, but our official language is English. • We eat corn, rice, chicken, wild fruit, and nuts. • We play soccer and rugby.

HATANI TSUSES, 10

How Namibia Looks Like

Wow! Namibian deserts are beautiful
Plus our pretty and beautiful trees
And animals and the people
Are all so kind with guests
And they always feel free
And happy.
We also love
The city of Windhoek.
And I thank you for coming!

ESTER AKWEENDA, 10

How Namibia looks like

Wow! Namibians deserts are beautiful

plus our pretty and beautiful trees
a
and animals and the people
a
are so kind with guests

and they always feel free

and happy. We also love

the city of Windhoek.

And I thank you for
coming!

Nauru | Oceania

We speak Nauruan and English. • We eat rice, canned and frozen foods, fish, and coconut. • We play Australian-rules football.

HEARTSON SCOTTY, 11

I love Nauru because in school
They teach me how to read and write
And in church I hear music
And the pastor talks loudly
And I have friends who are good to me
And we play games
I love shopping with my friends
And I love swimming in the sea
And my favorite pets in Nauru
Are a cat and a dog.

ANCINE DAGEAGO, 11

A Auwe bwiō Naoero bwe dōgin wōn
kereri ŋama Wereriō reitsin me-tor.
Me a gona riaŋ me kaiyat angogen Gott
iat tondak.
Tsimine bet estore ao matw matuwal
Me ma ibibogin bet ogo yan
wōn wited Naoero
A gona bet oranga
butsi me robor.

256

Nepal | Asia

We speak Nepali. • We eat *dal bhaat* (rice and lentil soup), curried vegetables, goat, chicken, and yogurt. • We play soccer, volleyball, and badminton.

KRISHNA TAMANG, 13

My Country Nepal

My country Nepal will always stand tall
Here there are many Himalayan peaks
The rivers and streams always sing songs
The danphe* and munal* dance to their tune

There are many peaks in the verdant mountains
Clumps of rhododendron adorn those peaks
The colorful flowers attract everyone's mind
And this is the wealth of my country

SAROJ RAI, 12

* Multicolored pheasants of Nepal

मेरो देश नेपाल

मेरो देश नेपाल सधैं रहन्छ उच्च
पाहाँ छन् हिमालका धेरै-धेरै चुच्चा
नदी ताला खोलाले सधैं गीत गाउँछ
त्यही गीत सुनेर डाप्ने मुनाल नाच्छन्

हरियाली पहाडमा धेरै छ ट्प्पा
त्यहि पहाडका ट्प्पामा लालीगुराँसका झुप्पा
रङ्गीचङ्गी फुलने तान्छ सबको मन
पहि हो मेरो देश नेपालकी धन

Netherlands | Europe

We speak Dutch. • We eat Dutch cheese, *kroket* (deep-fried sausage), and *groentesoep* (vegetable soup). • We play soccer, tennis, and field hockey.

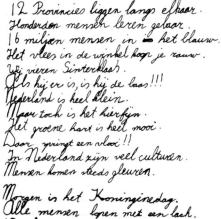

JENNY, 12

12 Provincies liggen langs elkaar.
Honderden mensen leren gebaar.
16 miljoen mensen in het blauw.
Het vlees in de winkel koop je rauw.
Wij vieren Sinterklaas.
Als hij er is, is hij de baas!!!
Nederland is heel klein.
Maar toch is het hier fijn.
Het groene hart is heel mooi.
Daar springt een vlooi!!
In Nederland zijn veel culturen.
Mensen komen steeds gluren.

Morgen is het Koninginnedag.
Alle mensen lopen met een lach.
15 molens in een wei.
Mensen wachten in de rij.
16 miljoen mensen op een stuk aarde.
Hoewel het weer klaarde.
Ik gebruik nu gebaar want,
Mijn gedicht is nu klaar!!!

Twelve provinces next to each other
Hundreds of people learning to move.
Sixteen million people in blue
We buy our raw meat at the supermarket.
We celebrate Saint Nicholas*.
When he is there, he is the boss!!!

The Netherlands are very small.
But life there is very good.
The green heart is very beautiful.
It even has a jumping flee!!
In the Netherlands there are many cultures.
People come and visit.

Tomorrow is the queen's celebration.
Everyone smiles happily.
Fifteen windmills in a meadow.
People waiting and queuing.
Sixteen million people on a piece of land.
Although the sky is getting clear.
I now use the gesture, because
My poem is finished!!!   JAÍRO, 11

* Saint Nicholas's Eve (December 5th) is an important gift-giving day for Dutch children

New Zealand | Oceania

We speak English and Maori. • We eat seafood, fruit and vegetables, roasted lamb, and ice cream. • We play rugby, soccer, cricket, and field hockey.

ZOE VAUNOIS, 9

New Zealand

New Zealand is a wonderful country
The scenery is blue and green
We are an undiscovered land for people
like you and me
The citizens have a friendly smile
to welcome you here.
We are hard-working kiwis*
At any time of the year
We have forests, farmers, and animals
Happy and healthy and bright so on
New Zealand you should shed some light

HELENA DOUGLAS THOMSON, 10

*The kiwi bird is the national symbol for New Zealand, and New Zealanders are generally called "kiwis"

New Zealand
New Zealand is a
wonderful Country the
Scenery is blue and green
we are an undisrovered
land for peole like you
and me. the Citizens have
a friendly smile waiting
to welcome you here we
are hard working Kiwis
at any time of the year
We have forests farmers and
Animals Happy and healthy
and bright so on
New Zealand you should
shed some light.

Nicaragua | Central America

We speak Spanish. • We eat beans and rice, tortillas, corn, tropical fruits, and *plátanos* (fried plantains). • We play baseball, soccer, and basketball.

GEOVANNY MAIRENA PAZ, 11

Mi tierra Nicaragua.

Yo vivo en un País, con lindas tierras y valles,
Yo vivo en un País, con lindos juegos y bailes.

Se llama Nicaragua, así se llama mi tierra,
tiene muchas leyendas, tiene muchos bailes.

Yo no cambiaria, a mi tierra Nicaragua,
Pues ella fue la que me vio nacer,
Yo no dejaria, que nadie me separara
de mi tierra Nicaragua, pues en ella
yo he de crecer y ahi morir.

Juego, canto y baila eso es lo
que puedo hacer, apriendo en la
escuela muchas cosas de mi
tierra, hay mi Nicaragua, yo ya
no se que hacer, espero que
Dios te guarde di y ami, tambien.

My Land Nicaragua

I live in a country, with pretty lands and valleys
I live in a country, with nice games and dances
Its name is Nicaragua, that's how my land is named,
It has many legends, it has many dances.

I wouldn't exchange my land Nicaragua
Because it is the one that saw me born
I wouldn't let anybody separate me
From my land Nicaragua, because in it
I shall grow and there I will die.

I play, sing, and dance
That's what I can do,
I learn in school many things about my land,
Ay! My Nicaragua I don't know what to do anymore,
I hope God saves you and me too.

MARIA DIAZ RODRIGUEZ, 12

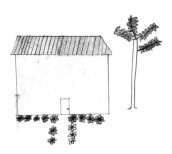

Niger | Africa

We speak many languages, but our official language is French. • We eat beans, corn, rice, and mangoes. • We play soccer, and we like camel racing.

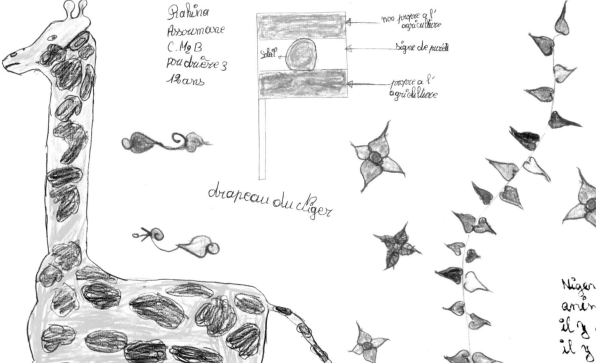

Rahina
Assoumane
C.M₂ B
pou driène 3
12 ans

Solal

non propre a l'agriculture

signe de pureté

propre a l'agriculture

drapeau du Niger

Niger is a country
There are people
And wild animals
Niger is a poor country
There are cars on the street, which roll
There are camels in the desert, which walk
There are sheep that eat food
Nigerians dance on the road
There are little girls who eat fruits.
I love my country!

RABI SAMI, 11

Niger est un pays il y a des personnes des animaux sauvage. Le Niger est un pays pauvre. Il y a des voiture sur la route qui roule. il y a des chameaux dans le desert qui marché. il y a des mouton qui mange des nourriture. il y a les nigeria qui danse sur la route. il y a de petite filles qui mange du fruits. J'aime mon pays.

MADJID ABOUBACAR MAMANE, 10

266

Nigeria | Africa

We speak many languages, but our official language is English. • We eat rice, fish, chicken, and vegetables. • We play soccer, polo, and cricket.

PATRICIA, AMINA, VICTOR, TEMPLE, HENRY, CHIOMA, AND NATHANIEL, 12

My Country

My country Nigeria
All hail Nigeria,
My blessed and blossoming country,
Nigeria, the giant of Africa.

Full of resources, both natural and human,
Strategically positioned for optimum achievement.

I am happy to have Africa
But better still Nigeria.

I am proud of my country,
United we stand with various tribes and tongues,
For we have found unity in our diversities
Most fascinating of all is our rich culture
Thrilling and entertaining.

You want to borrow from us?
You are welcome!
Why?
Because we are ready to share!

The lord is our strength in Nigeria,
God bless our country Nigeria.

FATIH, FATIMAH, PHILIP, AUGUSTINA,
ADAM, JOHN, AND EFOSA, 12

Norway | Europe

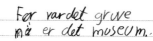

INGRID KLEMMETVOLD, 10

Før var det gruve
nå er det museum.

Før var det skole
nå er det museum.

Før brukter dem Hest
nå bruker dem bil.

Før brukte dem radio
nå bruke vi teve.

Før Hørte de på Elvis presleg
na Hører de på teh kids.

Før spist de grøt
nå spist de taco.

Before there was a mine
Now there is a museum

Before there was a school
Now there is a museum

Before they used horses
Now they use cars

Before they listened to the radio
Now we watch TV

Before they listened to Elvis Presley
Now they listen to the Kids

Before they ate porridge
Now they eat tacos

MAREN KIKHUS, 9

Oman

Asia (Middle East)

We speak many languages, but our official language is Arabic. • We eat rice, chicken, lamb, goat, seafood, fruit, and mushrooms. • We play soccer.

STUDENTS OF AL BASAYR SCHOOL, 10

في عمان وادي جميلة
في عمان حديقة نظيفة وجميلة كثيرة
في عمان مدارس
في عمان المتلحف كثيرة
في عمان الناس كثيرون
في عمان الفنادق كثيرة
في عمان جمال كثيرة
في عمان جمال كبيرة
في عمان سلاحف كثيرة
أحبوكي يا عمان يا الأرض جمال

In Oman there's a beautiful valley
In Oman there are clean and beautiful gardens
In Oman there are lots of schools
In Oman there are many museums
In Oman there are many people
In Oman there are many hotels
In Oman there are many camels
In Oman there are big camels
In Oman there are many turtles
I love you Oman, oh land of beauty

ILYAS, 10

Pakistan | Asia

We speak many languages, but mostly English and Urdu. • We eat pita bread, yogurt, and spicy rice. • We play cricket, field hockey, and squash.

My Land

We are the stars of this land
We are loved by all
We are the little children of Pakistan
The color of the morning is by us

By us is the evening so bright
We are the stars of this land
We are a whiff of fragrance we are the shears of light
When we grow old we will do good deeds

One day we will bring laurels to our country
We will get the education and earn the good name
We are the stars of this earth
We respect our elders
We love the young ones
We have great regard for the teachers
We study with an earnest heart
We are the stars of this land
We are loved by all.

MADEEHA ASLAM, 11

MADIHA, 12

میری دھرتی

ہم دھرتی کے تارے
سب کو لگیں ہم پیارے

ہم ہیں ننھے منے بچے پاکستان
ہم سے ہے یہ رنگیں ہم سے صبح کی شان

ہم دھرتی کے تارے
ہم خوشبو کے جھونکے ہم کرنوں کے دھارے

ہم کے بڑے ہوں گے دنیا میں اچھے کام کریں گے بڑھک سا
اپنے ملن کا نام دنیا روشن نام کریں گے سا

ہم ادیب بنیں گے بڑھک کے سب
ہم دھرتی کے تارے

ہم بڑوں کی عزت کرتے ہیں
ہم چھوٹوں سے پیار کرتے ہیں

ہم اپنے استاندکا احترام کرتے ہیں
ہم دل لگا کر پڑھتے ہیں

ہم دھرتی کے تارے
سب کو لگیں ہم پیارے

مدیحہ اسلم

Palau | Oceania

We speak Palauan and English. • We eat cassava, yams, fish, rice, pizza, bananas, and papayas. • We play basketball, baseball, and softball.

We Love Palau

We love Palau in our own way
Some may say Palau is paradise
We say it has a beautiful sunrise
Palau has always amazed the world
With its beautiful nature
Palau, a nation of culture

STUDENTS OF KOROR PRIMARY SCHOOL, 11

Palau has a Flag with two colors. The yellow circle inside is just like the Sun and the blue color Outside is the color of the ocean.

"We love Palau"
We love Palau in our own way,
Some may say Palau is paradise
We say it has a beautiful sunrise
Palau has always amazed the world with its beautiful nature,
Palau a nation of culture.

MORISANG, CHARITY, LALII, DURAIMU, TURANG, MARIO, MARVIN, DAREK, TEXXON, AND ARANT, 12

Panama | Central America

We speak Spanish and English. • We eat rice, fish, beans, plantains, and *sancocho* (chicken soup). • We play soccer, baseball, and basketball.

ALABRADES DE LEON, 9

Long live Panama
Now and forever, long live Panama

Very early when I wake up
I greet
And happily say good morning
To my parents

Long live Panama
Now and forever, long live Panama

Please small key
Open the door anytime
Anytime I want, and anytime I ask
You for something

Long live Panama
Now and forever, long live Panama

KATHERINE GUSTAVINO, 10

coro
Qué viva viva panamá
y haora vivapanama
o
muy temprano al levantarme
voy contento a saludar a
desirle buenos dias a mi
Dios y a mis papas.
o
qué viva viva panamá y
baora viva panama.
o
por favor llavesita
que abre puerta sencesa
cuando quiero y cuando pido
una cosa suplicar.
o
coro.

Papua New Guinea | Oceania

We speak more than 800 languages, but mostly Melanesian Pidgin, English, and Motu. • We eat seafood, coconuts, and wild pigs. • We play rugby.

My country has mountains
My country has creeks
My country has rivers
So wide and so big.

My country has lakes
My country has springs
My country has swamps
With colorful lillies.

My country has caves
My country has bats
My country has flowers
In blooming bright colors.

My country has snakes
My country has birds
My country has butterflies
That have birdlike wings.

And last of all,
My country has people
like you and me.

ROLLY ELIVAP, 12

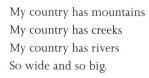

KOKENU MAKITA, 12

MY COUNTRY HAS MOUNTAINS
MY COUNTRY HAS CREEKS
MY COUNTRY HAS RIVERS
SO WIDE AND SO BIG.

MY COUNTRY HAS LAKES
MY COUNTRY HAS SPRINGS
MY COUNTRY HAS SWAMPS
WITH COLOURFUL LILLIES.

MY COUNTRY HAS CAVES
MY COUNTRY HAS BATS
MY COUNTRY HAS FLOURS
IN BLOOMING BRIGHT COLOURS

MY COUNTRY HAS SNAKES
MY COUNTRY HAS BIRDS
MY COUNTRY HAS BUTTERFLIES
THAT HAVE BIRD LIKE WINGS.

AND LAST OF ALL, MY COUNTRY HAS
PEOPLE LIKE YOU AND ME.

Paraguay | South America

We speak Spanish and Guaraní. • We eat cornbread, tortillas, *empanadas* (meat or vegetable turnovers), and fruit. • We play soccer and volleyball.

TANIA FRANCO, 11

Paraguay

Paraguay is a small country
But very beautiful
And every color of the flag
Has its own meaning.
Red for justice,
White for peace,
Blue for freedom
There is nothing like the
Paraguayan flag.
And local food is:
Sopa paraguaya*, mbeju**,
Pastel mandio***
And many more
Its typical games are the
tiquichuela****, the pandorga*****,
and many more.
Paraguay has two languages:
Guaraní and Spanish.
There are also a lot of typical clothes,
like Ao po'i******, the ñanduti*******,
    and many more.

MARIA MAGDALENA OCAMPOS, 12

* A cake made of corn flour
** Starch cake made of manioc (cassava) flour, a solid sample of the Paraguayan gastronomy
*** Stuffed pastry made of manioc (cassava) flour
**** Knucklebones
***** Kite
****** Embroidered fabric; *Ao* means clothing and *po'i* means handmade
******* Lace adorning traditional clothes

Peru | South America

We speak Spanish, Quechua, and Aymara. • We eat rice and *ceviche* (raw seafood dish marinated in lime). • We play soccer, basketball, and volleyball.

To My Peru

My country is big and beautiful
People are loving and affectionate
Its sites are beautiful and fantastic
Machu Picchu* is the peoples' pride and heart
Its dishes are delicious because when you think about them,
You want to have some, like ceviche**, made with fish, spicy and delicious
The colors of our flag represent:
Red, the blood shed by innocent heroes who defended our country,
White, peace, which reigns among Peruvian people
That is why we tell the place where we were born
Long live Peru! And let's hope it keeps on growing along with the kids,
who are the future of the country.

ARACELLI REYME ALEGRIA, 15

* Pre-Columbian Inca site located 2,430 meters above sea level
** Citrus and chile marinated seafood appetizer

A Mi Perú

Mi país es grande y bello,
la gente es armoniosa y cariñosa.
Sus sitios son hermosos y estupendos.
Machu-Picchu es el orgullo y el
corazón de la gente
Sus platos deliciosos porq' apenas se te
vienen a la mente te probocas como el cebiche a base de pesca'
picante y delicioso.
        Los colores de su bandera representan,
        rojo, la sangre q' derramaron los héroes por
        su inocencia y por defender a nuestra patria,
blanco, la paz q' hay entre los peruanos.
Por eso nosotros le decimos al lugar donde nacimos
        ¡Viva el Perú! y q' sigua creciendo con los
        niños, q' son el futuro del país.

JANIN SARANGA, 9

284

Philippines | Asia

We speak English and Filipino. • We eat rice, seafood, goat, tropical fruits, and *adobo* (chicken and pork stew). • We play basketball and volleyball.

What I want to achieve
Is a country full of peace
You'll be in awe
When you see it:

Surroundings so clean,
Not vexing,
Waste will be placed in the proper place
And everyone will be truly cheery

If my dream is fulfilled
For sure our land will be in bliss
More tourists will come
And everyone will be thriving

Everything will be easy to achieve
If only we work hard for it
So do not forget what has been said:
Anything can be done!

AKITO MARC T. IRAVE JR., 12

Ang Pangarap Ko
Sa Bayan Ko

Ang gusto kung makamtan
   Bansang may kapayapaan
Na kung iyong malinpa
   Ay kahanga-hanga

Paligid na malinis
   At hindi yaong nakakainis
Basura'y itapon sa tamang lagayan
   Ng ang lahat pati tayo'y masiyahan

Kung ang pangarap ko ay makamtan
   Tiyak ding sisigla itong aking bayan
Darami ang mga dayuhan
   At dahil dito maaari tayong yumaman

Ang lahat naman ay madali nating kokamtin
   Basta't pagsikapan natin
Kaya huwag kaligtaan ang aking binilin
   Na ang lahat ay kaya nating abutin

LALLY R. ROSALES, 11

Poland | Europe

We speak Polish. • We eat soup, potatoes, *pierogi* (stuffed dumplings), and various pastries. • We play soccer, basketball, volleyball, and table tennis.

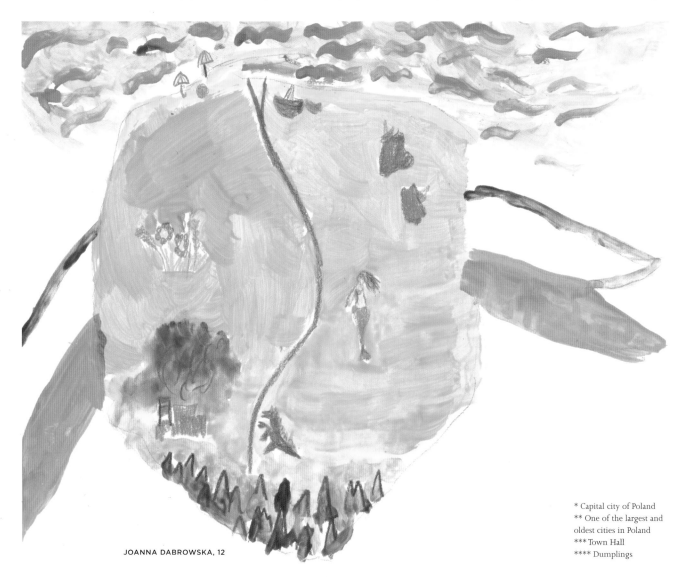

JOANNA DABROWSKA, 12

W Polsce piękny jest krajobraz,
trochę gór i trochę morza.
Kwiatów pełne są przestrzenie,
noi zato ją kochamy.
Szkoły piękne są jak domy,
i Warszawa duża jest.
Kraków piękne ma zabytki,
sukiennice i wieżyczki.
Świętych bardzo dużo mamy,
i pierogów dużo jemy.
Patron każdy ma opiekę,
po stra zak, góral no i górnik.
To jest Polska ma kochana,
dziś, wczoraj i medwczoraj.

In Poland, there are beautiful landscapes,
Some mountains and some sea,
Territories full of flowers
And for all that, we love Poland.
Schools are as beautiful as the houses
And Warsaw* is big.
Krakow** has beautiful monuments:
The Sukiennice*** and other towers.
We have a lot of saints
And we eat a lot of pierogi****.
Our Protector takes care:
Firemen, people from mountains, and miners.
It is Poland I have loved
Today, yesterday, and the day before yesterday.

* Capital city of Poland
** One of the largest and oldest cities in Poland
*** Town Hall
**** Dumplings

WRONIKA KARSKA, 9

Portugal | Europe

We speak Portuguese. • We eat soup, meat, fruit and vegetables, *bacalhau* (dried salt cod), and a variety of sweets. • We play soccer and basketball.

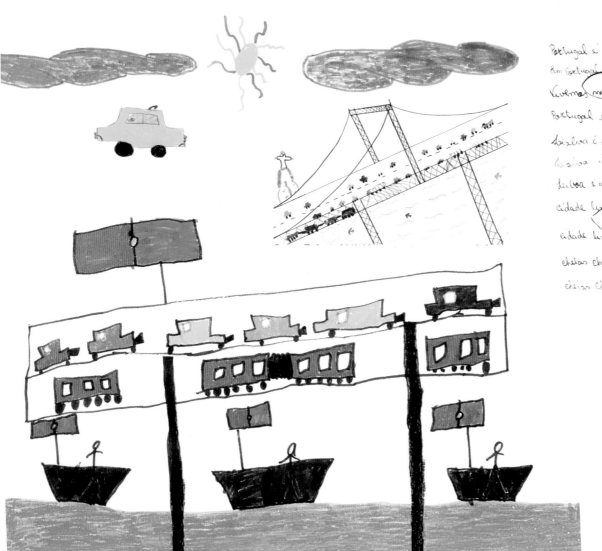

Portugal é mais linda que uma flor.
Em Portugal nasceu a liberdade.
Vivemos num País maravilhoso é Portugal
Portugal é a nossa felicidade.
Lisboa é a nossa cidade
Lisboa é a nossa cidade
Lisboa é a capital do meu amado Portugal
cidade linda é maravilhosa
cidade linda é Lisboa é mais linda que uma papoila
chelas chelinhas se não fosses tu não havia estrelinhas
chelas Chelinhas se não fosses tu não viria

MADALENA, 9

Portugal is more beautiful than a flower
Freedom was born in Portugal
We live in a marvelous country, it is Portugal
Portugal is our happiness
Lisbon is our city
Lisbon is the capital of our beloved Portugal
Beautiful and marvelous city,
Lisbon, nice city, nicer than a poppy
Chelas*, small Chelas, if you didn't exist,
There wouldn't be any star
Chelas, small Chelas, if you didn't exist,
I wouldn't be able to live.

NEUZA SANCHES, 10

* Residential district in the suburbs of Lisbon

Qatar | Asia (Middle East)

We speak Arabic and English. • We eat rice, flat bread, fish, lamb, yogurt, and many vegetables. • We play soccer and basketball, and like camel racing.

Qatar is my country
Qatar is my home
Everyday before I sleep
I know that I am not alone
Because all the people that I love
Live in the country that's number one

With golden sands
And a sun that shone and shone
With tall buildings
That grew one by one
With lots of cars
And lines of traffic in the sun

There are lots of places
Where we can laugh and have fun
Even in the summer when it's hot
I smile to everyone
Because we all know
That Qatar is number one.

FATIMA HANI HUSSAIN, 11

HESSA NASSER, 9

Qatar is my country
Qatar is my home
Everyday before I sleep
I know that I am not alone.
because all the people that I love.
live in the country thats number one
with golden sands
and a sun that shone and shone
with tall buildings
that grew one by one
with lots of cars
and lines of traffic in the sun
there are lots of places
where we can laugh and have fun
even in the summer when its hot
I smile to everyone.
because we all know
that Qatar is number one.

Romania | Europe

We speak Romanian. • We eat *mititei* (spiced sausage), *mamaliga* (cornmeal mush), eggs, and soup. • We play soccer and we like gymnastics.

BARBU BIANCA, 12

Dear Romania

Dear pretty lady
Dressed up in three colors
You, the triumphant result
Of this brave people.

I respect and I cherish you
I owe you so much
If you should ever be in need
I'll be there for you.

I bow
In front of lady Romania
With the well chosen lucky number
Of the colors on the flag.

We take the blue in the sky
The yellow from the corn field crops
The red blood from our heroes
Three colors — a flag for us.

BARBU DIANA, 12

Dragă Românie,
Dragă Doamnă aranjată,
În trei colori îmbrăcată,
Rezultat triumfător
Al ăstui viteaz popor,

Te respect şi te stimez
Multe eu îţi datorez.
De vreodată-ţi vei dori,
În ajutor îţi voi veni.

Îmi pun jos pălăria
În faţa Doamnei România,
Ce-are cifra norocoasă
De la drapel bine-aleasă.

Luăm albastru de pe cer,
De la holde galben cer,
Roşu-i sânge de eroi,
Trei culori – steag pentru noi.

Russia | Eurasia

We speak Russian. • We eat *borscht* (vegetable soup), bread, potatoes, beets, pork, and chicken. • We play soccer and winter sports, like ice hockey.

BARBARA LEMRACHYK, 11

Wintry-Winter

So good is the winter snow,
So good is the skiing path,
So good is the winter forest
Under the glow of skies.

There is so much ice and snow;
Kids are coming out into the backyards
To make a snow-lady,
To make a snowman;
What a beautiful season,
So good is the winter!

DANIEL TENYAKOV, 12

«ЗИМУШКА-ЗИМА»

Как хорош зимний снег,
Как хорош лыжный бег,
Как хорош зимний лес
Под мерцанье небес.

Снега полно и льда,
Вышла во двор детвора,
Лепят снежную бабу,
Лепят снеговика;
Как прекрасна пора,
Как хороша зима!

Rwanda | Africa

We speak French, Kinyarwanda, and English. • We eat beans, *frites* (french fries), beef, bananas, and sweet potatoes. • We play soccer and basketball.

Rwanda

Rwanda is a beautiful country
The country of nice people
You can find forests, animals, hotels, and schools
In Rwanda there are trees
You can eat french fries and salad
You can see cars
You can see the nature
You can see colors
You can see the national flag
And us, dancing all together

LIONEL MBARUBUCYEYE, 8

NICOLE MUHAWENIMANA, 9

LE RWANDA
1-Le Rwanda est un beau pays
- Le pays des hommes gentils.
- On y trouver des forêts, des animaux, des hotels, des ecole
- Dans le Rwanda il y a des arbres.
- On y mange des frites, des la salades.
- On y voit des voitures.
- On y voit la nature.
- On y voit des couleurs
- Il y a le drapeau nationale
- On y danse tous ensemble

Saint Kitts & Nevis | Central America

We speak English. • We eat salt fish, dumplings, chicken, pork, rice, and fruit and vegetables. • We play cricket, soccer, basketball, and volleyball.

St. Kitts is my homeland
St. Kitts is my home
Everywhere you go in St. Kitts
You could see beautiful homes.
I love St. Kitts. Do you want to know why?
I am always happy when my mom is around.
She takes me to the beautiful historic sites around
And even to Basseterre*.
There is so much I can say about St. Kitts
But I'll make it short and sweet.
St. Kitts is the only place
To make you feel like me.

JEVAUGHN BROWN, 11

* Capital city of the Federation of Saint Kitts and Nevis

DIAHON JUNG AND JERREL WATTLEY, 9

St Kitts is my homeland
St Kitts is my home
Everywhere you go in ST Kitts you
could see beautiful homes
I love ST Kitts you want to know why
I am always happy when my moms
around
She takes me to the beautiful historic
sites around and even into Basseterre
town.
There is so much I can say about
ST Kitts but i'll make it short and
sweet.
ST Kitts is the only place to make
you feel like me.

Saint Lucia | Central America

We speak English. • We eat rice, peas, beef, chicken, fish, *conch* (mollusk), goat, and tropical fruits. • We play soccer and cricket.

St. Lucia

St. Lucia is a beautiful Isle
Where friendly people greet you with a smile
The tourists love the sunshine here.
And say it's the most beautiful.
They love the greenery that they see
And marvel at our ma-sav tree.
I love St. Lucia, it's my home land
It's blessed and was given by divine hand.
We call it Helen of the West.
Because the people are friendly and truly blessed.

DYLAN SINGH, 9

St. Lucia

St. Lucia is a beautiful Isle
Where friendly people greet you with a smile
The tourists love the sunshine here.
And say it's the most beautiful.
They love the greenery that they see
And marvel at our massav* tree.
I love St. Lucia, it's my homeland.
It's blessed and was given by divine hand.
We call it Helen of the West.
Because the people are friendly and truly blessed.

SABINA LABADIE, 9

* Local name of the Samaan or rain tree with low and large spreading branches

Saint Vincent & The Grenadines | Central America

We speak English. • We eat rice, bananas, pumpkins, plantains, and *boul-joul* (salted codfish with vegetables). • We play cricket, soccer, and squash.

ASHINI BEST, 10

Saint Vincent our island we hold with care, mountains, trees, and rivers of beauty we share, An enormous volcano and deep blue sea, an island full of treasure the world should see.

VAUGHAN RUSSELL, 10

St. Vincent Our island we hold with care, Mountains, trees and rivers of beauty we Share, An enormous volcano and deep blue Sea, An island Full of treasure the world Should See.

Samoa | Oceania

We speak Samoan and English. • We eat taro, seafood, chicken, tomatoes, limes, and pineapples. • We play rugby, basketball, and *kilikiti* (like cricket).

AGE-10

JACOB ANVAA, 10

Coconut Tree

If you want to know me
My name is coconut tree
All of my parts are good
For people who need food

I am so important,
Because some of my parts are exported
People like to make me as a ball
When some of my parts fall

My stem is brown but leaves are green
Everyone usually makes food from my cream
I was raised up by an eel,
And now the coconut is easy to peel.

TUPOSILIVA, 12

San Marino | Europe

We speak Italian. • We eat pasta, wild boar, seafood, and *piadina romagnola* (flat bread). • We play soccer and volleyball, and like skiing and cycling.

ANDREANI SARA AND DI SILVESTRI ELISA, 10

My Mountain

My mountain is high
When I look up to it
I feel
Safe and strong.

My mountain is imposing
As a king
It leans
Over the valley.

My mountain is very old
As time goes by
It has been a source
Of history and freedom.

My mountain is a friend
It was looking at me when I was born
And still today,
Makes me feel at home.

CECILIA BUSIGNANI, 10

Mio Monte

Alto è il mio monte
Guardando
Mi trasmette
Sicurezza e forza.

Maestoso è il mio monte
Come un re
Si mostra
Su tutta la vallata.

Antico è il mio monte
Nel tempo
Si è mostrato
Fonte di storia e libertà.

Amico è il mio monte,
Che mi ha visto nascere
E, ancor oggi,
Mi fa sentire a casa.

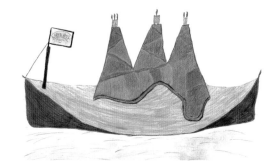

Sao Tome & Principe | Africa

We speak Portuguese. • We eat plantains, rice, beans, bread, pork, chicken, goat, duck, seafood, snails, and fruit and vegetables. • We play soccer.

Príncipe

S. Tomé

ALIMARY PATRICIA, 8

In the middle of the ocean
Lay two green islands.
Pure forests,
Natural beauties,
Visitors and many rains
Here you'll find everything you
like
Tasty fruits
Waterfalls, peaks, and mountains
Oh! And also pretty beaches
Good for sunbathing

BRUNO CARDOSO, 9

No meio do Oceano
Existem duas ilhas verdes
Florestas virgens
Beleza natural
Visitantes e muitas chuvas
Aqui tem tudo que gostas
Saborosos frutos
Cascatas, pcos e montanhas
Oh! também lindas praias
Bom pegar o sol.

Saudi Arabia | Asia (Middle East)

We speak Arabic. • We eat rice with lamb or chicken, seafood, vegetables, and we drink camel's milk. • We play volleyball, basketball, and soccer.

FAISAL AL YAHYA, 11

مملكة العز

مملكتنا يا مملكة العز والأسلام
رايتك الخضراء ما تنام يا مملكة الكنز
والعز واعها روأفكار يا وطن الحب عطرايا
كل حبة من التراب الثمين تعبر عن
حبك يا وطن العز

Kingdom of Pride

Our Kingdom oh kingdom of pride and Islam
Your flag green doesn't sleep, oh kingdom of treasure
And pride, people, and ideas.
Oh land of love with Jasmine's perfume
Every little grain of your precious sand expresses your love, land of pride.

MOHD BANDER AL SAUD, 11

Senegal | Africa

We speak many languages, but our official language is French. • We eat rice, poultry, fish, yogurt, and vegetables. • We play soccer and basketball.

carte afrique

CHEIKH FADEL SAKHO, 10

When you wake up in Senegal,
You see the sunrise
You hear the birds sing
Senegal has peace
But some other countries don't
But here there is peace
That is why I love Senegal
And I pray that peace in Senegal
Goes to other countries too.

KHALIFA CISSE, 10

quand tu te leve au Sénégal tu vois le Soleil
se leve. tu entend le chant des oiseaux.
le Senegal a la paie. Mais dans autres pays
il n'y a pas de paix. Mais ici il y a la paix
C'est pourquoi j'adore le Senegal. et je
prie pour que la paix qui est au Senegal
continue dans d'autres pays.

Serbia | Europe

We speak many languages, but mostly Serbian. • We eat *pasulj* (beans), roasted pork, lamb, and ice cream. • We play soccer, basketball, and volleyball.

My Town

I love it in autumn, when the leaves turn gold,
And in winter, when the wind blows,
I love it in spring, filled with thousands of colors,
And in summer, at Strand*, while I swim.

I love it at night, when the boulevards glow,
And in the morning, when it wakes from a dream,
I love its bridges and the blue Danube,
More than anything I love my town!

INIC DRAGANA, 10

* Beach on the Danube in the city of Novi Sad

MIAGEN POJOBUTH, 10

Seychelles | Africa

We speak English, French, and Creole.   •   We eat rice with most meals, seafood, chicken, and fruit.   •   We play soccer and *petanque* (lawn bowling).

JULIO MOREL, 11

My Country Seychelles

My country is very beautiful
We all live in unity, peacefully, in harmony.
In the district we all help to make it blossom
Together we live in harmony
Everywhere you go, you will see people helping
In all activities, we contribute somehow
But even if we don't manage to achieve what we want
We don't get desperate
Sometimes we are proud
When we help the world to be better
Even if the price of things is expensive
We don't get scared
Because with our prayer, God will guide this Paradise
To make it better.

VALENTINA VIDOT, 11

Sierra Leone | Africa

We speak English and Krio. • We eat rice with *plassas* (sauce), beans, fish, chicken, bush animals, and tropical fruits. • We play soccer and volleyball.

JAUDA A. FULLAH, 11

The Land of My Birth

Sweet Sierra Leone
Sweet Sierra Leone
Sierra Leone, the productive land
Where varieties of crops grow
I am proud of sweet potatoes
I am proud of cassava
The beautiful morning hours,
Seeing the beautiful inhabitants
Bringing varieties of crops grown in town
Oh sweet Sierra Leone
The productive land of my birth
Wherever I go I will never forget
My sweet country Sierra Leone

ABU B. MARRAH, 11

The Land of my birth

Sweet SierraLeone Sweet Sierra Leone
Sierra Leone the productive Land, Where variety
of Crops grown, I am proud of Sweet potato,
I am proud of Cassava. The beautiful morning
hours Seeing the beautiful inhabitant bringing
variety of Crops grown in town Oh Sweet
Sierra Leone. The productive Land of my birth
Where ever I go I will never forget My
Sweet Country Sierra Leone.

Singapore | Asia

We speak Malay, Chinese, Tamil, and English. • We eat rice, seafood, *dim sum* (Chinese dumplings), and Indian bread. • We play soccer and badminton.

LIN XIN YAN, 10

Clean...Green...

Clean ...Green ...Clean ...Green ...
Is all that you can see!
Clean ...Green ...Clean ...Green ...
Is all for you and me!

Clean ...Green ...Clean ...Green ...
Is all that you can dream!
Clean ...Green ...Clean ...Green ...
It's a lovely thing for me!

Clean ...Green ...Clean ...Green ...
For all your house and garden needs ...

STUDENTS OF SAINT STEPHEN SCHOOL, 10

Clean....Green....

Clean   Green   Clean   Green
Is all that you can see!
Clean   Green   Clean   Green
Is all for you and me!

Clean   Green   Clean   Green
Is all that you can dream!
Clean   Green   Clean   Green
It's a lovely thing for me!

Clean & Green
For all your house and garden needs

Slovakia | Europe

We speak Slovak. • We eat breaded steak and potatoes, cabbage, carrots, pasta, soup, and fruit. • We play soccer, ice hockey, and tennis.

My Motherland!

Slovakia is very beautiful,
I am writing a poem about it,
Slovakia is my motherland,
Where I like to grow.

In Slovakia,
There are a lot of cars, in the capital,
In Zvolen*, there is a castle
With a nice garden.

Our Tatras**, our honor,
Congratulate us.
And near Vah, there are many people
We watch as it (the river) flows.

BARBORA SIMKOVICOVÁ, 9

* Ancient town with a historical center and a castle
** Mountain range, natural border between Slovakia and Poland

Moja rodná zem
Slovensko je veľmi krásne,
píšem o ňom túto báseň.
Slovensko je moja vlasť,
v ktorej budem rada rásť.

Na Slovensku v hlavnom meste,
jazdí veľa áut po ceste.
Vo Zvolene hrad,
a v ňom pekný sad.

Naše Tatry, naša česť,
gratulujte na počesť.
a pri Váhu veľa ľudí,
hladíme naň ako prúdi.

LUKAS LJUBOVIC, 9

324

Slovenia | Europe

We speak Slovene. • We eat soup, wild berries, sausages, dried fruit, and strudels. • We play ice hockey, basketball, volleyball, and soccer.

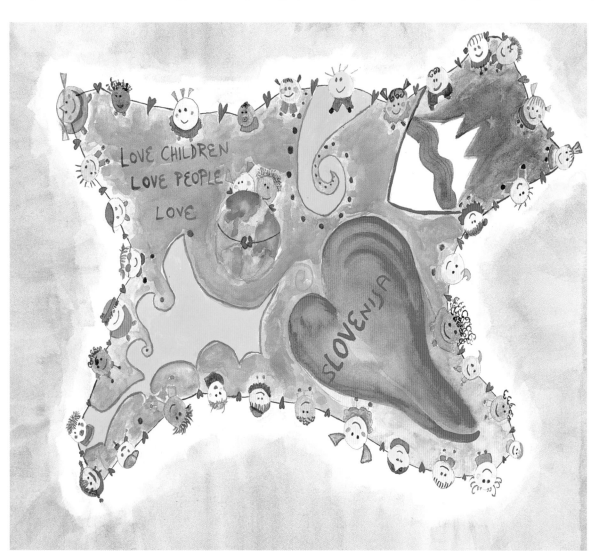

ENYA BELAK, 14

It's got mountains,
it's got water,
it's got roads,
it's got forests,
it's got bridges,
it's got towns,
market towns and villages.
This is a small,
safe, happy country.
Which country is this?
This is SLOVENIA.

NEZA BREGAR, 13

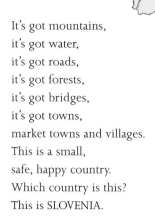

Ima gore,
ima vode,
ima morje,
ima ceste,
ima gozdove,
ima mostove,
ima mesta,
trge in vasi.
To je majhna,
varna, srečna dežela.
Le katera dežela je to?
To je SLOVEnija.

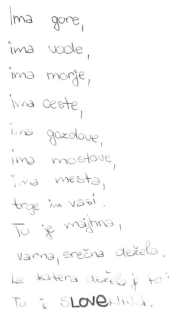

326

Solomon Islands | Oceania

We speak many languages, but our official language is English. • We eat cassava, taro, yams, fish, nuts, and tropical fruits. • We play soccer.

PADDLE, PADDLE

Paddle, Paddle, Paddle,
This is What We do,
paddle, paddle, paddle
Paddle Our Canoe.
The strong wind is blowing
The darks waves are rolling
Home we are going,
Paddling Our Canoe.

Paddle, Paddle

Paddle, paddle, paddle.
This is what we do
Paddle, paddle, paddle.
Paddle our canoe.
The strong wind is blowing
The dark waves are rolling
Home we are going,
Paddling our canoe.

STUDENTS OF ST. NICOLAS SCHOOL, 9

REMMEY, 9

Somalia | Africa

We speak Somali. • We eat corn, camel and goat milk, yogurt, pancakes, beans, tropical fruits, and a few vegetables. • We play soccer.

About the cultural behaviors:
Don't make our land a desert
Our religion is Islam, and we should follow what it says!
We are people with a culture,
We are people with a heartbeat,
We are people with the culture of sharing
Care for it! Look after our culture!
Don't follow the bad ways of life that mislead you
Look after our Somalian culture!

SAAMIYA AXMED, 15

> hanabaad juurin dhazanko ha raacin Shirarue hale
> dinteenoo islaamoo annaa wiirtaa raacay
> Waxaanalay dad dhazanoo caadigo amaare
> naaliyaa naaliyaa Walaalayaal naalirja
> jahawareerka dunclaa ha raacina Walaalay
> dhazari reer jalbeediyo fikradah jalaadecd
> haraacinaa naaliya dhazankeena soomaali Land
> soomaatyeey loosoo haraacinaa dhazankaa ree
> yurub

KHADRA AXMED, 16

South Africa | Africa

We speak Afrikaans and English. • We eat roast beef or lamb, potatoes, curries, pickled fish, and vegetables. • We play soccer, rugby, and cricket.

I know a place in Africa
Where the trees dress the earth in a coat of green.
Where the lions roar and the springboks leap,
Where the sound of drums beat in my ears.

I know a place in Africa
Where elephants pound with their mighty feet.
Where I can hear the chirping of the birds in the trees.
Where a journey starts and never ends …
This is South Africa.

HEMAL PRAG, 10

LIZEN PAN, 10

332

Spain | Europe

We speak Castilian Spanish, Catalan, Galician, and Basque. • We eat chicken, seafood, rice, and *gazpacho* (cold vegetable soup). • We play soccer.

Por una gota de agua un mundo

Zaragoza

MARTA MORENA, 9

The Countryside

The countryside is pretty when it is sunny
Allowing plants to grow with love
And when the flowers bloom
Like a carpet of colors
Filling the air with scents
It makes shepherds happy.
But is a pity that where I live
There are neither flowers nor colors,
Only smelly exhausts
from trucks and cars.

SILVIA, 10

El campo es bonito con sol
para que las plantas crezcan con amor
y cuando nacen las flores
parece una alfombra de colores
que llenan el aire de olores
para alegrar a los pastores
la pena es que donde vivo yo
no hay flores, ni colores
solo hay malos olores
a coches y a camiones.

Sri Lanka | Asia

We speak Sinhala, Tamil, and English. • We eat rice, curries, fish, nuts, and *pol sambol* (spiced coconut). • We play cricket, soccer, and table tennis.

DINITHI NAVODYA LANAROL, 11

My Country

Small land surrounded by the great sea.
Smaller spot in the world map.
It's called Sri Lanka.
It's the victorious land.
It's filled with waterfalls and rivers.
Beautiful flowers bring their fragrance.
We can hear the sound of various animals.
Victory for my great country forever.

VINUJA VIHANSITH JAYASINHE, 9

මගේ රට

වටපිටින් වට වුනු තුඩා මුහ.
ලෝක කිතියේ පුංචි තිතක.
ශ්‍රී ලංකා යනු ඒකා නාමි.
පුරුම්රුවන් රට ලඟු මිහ.
ලියඅඳල ගඟා පිරි තිබි.
ලස්සන වට වල් පිටි සැලේ.
ගොයොක් තුන්හේ තඹ ඇසේ.
මගේ පුංචි රට දිනේ දිනේ.

Sudan | Africa

We speak Arabic, English, and Dinka. • We eat beef, chicken, peanut butter, and fruit and vegetables. • We play soccer, basketball, and volleyball.

ما أحد البلاد بلاد ي صنيب رمشة
عيد بلاد نا أنه م هالي بلاد الخير دائفة
وهدي هنقان محبه وحمد بني
محطفك حب الوطن طالي هو حب
السودان ثروا قوميني ولا نبيعه
من وطنك تحس م يال شمسي
و ما خك ما سشوب بلد ولاك يشحرم
الاطفا بلاد ي فرح الحب والحشفوى
بلا د ي شجرة وه ار ف نشمسي

SABA MUBARAK, 10

Sudan is the Shelter

How beautiful the country is
The country of nostalgia and surprise
The eye of my country is the one of a father, of a mother
The country of good and grandeur
The Mahadi* showered us his love
There is no love, no affection, such as the love and affection of our homeland
Sudan is a national wealth and we will never sell it
Inside your borders I feel the sun of my country
I swear in your name, that you don't look like any other in the world
You don't hesitate to give the children of my country
Happiness, love, and faith
My country is a tree, which shadow extends everywhere

HAGER ADAM, 10

* Religious and political leader (1844–1885), founder of the vast
Islamic Empire, extending from the Red Sea to the center of Africa

338

Suriname | South America

We speak Dutch, Sranan Tongo, and English.　•　We eat rice, *bami* (Javanese noodle dish), and tropical fruits.　•　We play soccer and basketball.

GWENDELIEN ALBOLTOL, 12

Suriname is a blessed country
With a huge forest and many rivers
And in these beautiful rivers, there are beautiful fish
There are delicious fish
Such as piring, krobia, toekoenari, wapoe, mooipie*
But there are also beautiful fish you cannot eat
Like the joembo and snoekoe
That's why I say Suriname is beautiful:
Not only because of the fish and trees
But also because of the flowers
That you can put at home
Or receive as a birthday present.

ROSLIE KENTIE, 11

* Freshwater fish of Suriname

Sanan se wan Blex kondre
naga somens wiri naga samens
liba. Sen liba mooi, dipi din
abi mooi visi.

Din abi Soloi-Soloi visi solche
piling, krobya, loegoenali, abongonie,
wakoe, anga moipi visi

goe abi visi sie-si (mooi) noi
m nehan sooi ike snochoe nanga
Jombo sen visi si di nai nehan sen

sou mike mie ecki Sanan
mooi liba as a, abi mooi Sani
eke visi naga lon, nango mooi
bloem si soe Sa poli awsoe
aga ie sama vorjalie

340

Swaziland | Africa

We speak SiSwati and English. • We eat corn, beans, mashed potatoes, and fruit and vegetables. • We play soccer, tennis, squash, volleyball, and golf.

NKOSIKHONA DLAMINI, 11

My Country

My country is in Africa
It is a land locked country
My country is beatyfull
It is a Peasefull country

That shakes clouds of the sky
There are singers in swaziland
My Country is full of green mountains.
There are small animals and birds that fly.
Shall I compere you to thurnder
Swaziland maight be small

My country is in Africa
It is a landlocked country
My country is beautiful
It is a peaceful country
That shakes clouds of the sky
There are singers in Swaziland
My country is full of green mountains
There are small animals and birds that fly
Shall I compare you to thunder?
Swaziland might be small

LUNGILE SHONGWE, 12

342

Sweden | Europe

We speak Swedish. • We eat seafood, meatballs, *fil* (yogurt), and fruit and vegetables. • We play soccer, tennis, golf, and winter sports like ice hockey.

AMANDA, 12

My name is Sara and I will tell you about Sweden.
The sun is warm, the sea is cool, nature is
beautiful and everything is fantastic.
Children go to school five hours a day and get a
good education. You would be happy if you
went to school here.
Wait and see what an enchanted place
can offer. You would love this place.
School is educational, nature is the best.
Grass and flowers are the best things I know.

SARA, 11

Switzerland | Europe

We speak German, French, Italian, and Romansch.   •   We eat meat, potatoes, leek soup, and fish.   •   We play soccer, but we also like cycling and hiking.

MELANIE OPPLIGER, 13

Switzerland

Switzerland is big
And the cheese is splendid
In Switzerland we study the verb
And in our free time
We go to the mountain
Cows are big,
And squirrels are fit
Cheese is good,
And we are very courageous
At school we learn a lot,
About the good old style
Nature is wonderful,
And there are lots of birds
And if Switzerland is still healthy,
Tomorrow we'll give it another round

SARINA, MAJA,
CARMEN,
AND NINA, 12

Die Schweiz ist gross,
und der Käse ist Famos.
In der Schweiz büffelt man um
das Verb, und in der Freizeit
geht man auf den Berg.
Die Kühe sind dick, und
die Eichörnchen sind fit.
Der Käse ist gut, und wir
haben grossen mut. In der
Schule lernen wir viel, über
den guten alten Stil. Die
Natur ist wunderbar, und es
gibt eine grosse Vogelschar.
Und ist die Schweiz noch
so gesund, geht es uns
morgen wieder rund.

Syria | Asia (Middle East)

We speak Arabic. • We eat lamb, hummus, *mutable* (mashed eggplant), bread, and fruit. • We play soccer, basketball, and volleyball.

SARAH SAFI, 10

حبه ملئ فؤادي   جنة الدنيا وطني

حنه للعين رائي   ريحه في كل واد

في الكهوف والغابي

جمالنيقات الرياض   حنه للعين باد

بين أعناب و زهر

حنه للعين يري   في الصفاء يجري

في الجبال والتلال

حبه ملئ فؤادي   جنة الدنيا وطني

My country is a paradise in the world
Its wind blows in every valley

In caves and gardens
In the finest ones

It runs as water
It spreads like perfume

Over the mountains and the hills
My country is the world's paradise

Its love fills my heart
Its beauty is clear to the eye

In streams and small gardens
Its beauty is clear to the eye

Between plants and flowers
Its beauty is clear to the eye

Its love fills my heart.

MOHAMMED JOUDEH, 11

348

Tajikistan | Asia

We speak Tajik and Russian. • We eat beef, mutton, chicken, fruit and vegetables, yogurt, and nuts. • We play soccer, basketball, and tennis.

MARUFJON FAIZIBOEV, 11

Tajikistan is beautiful
During Navruz* national holiday
People wear traditional clothes
Women wear traditional dresses
There are many mountains in Tajikistan
People go on holidays during the summer
People pick up cotton in autumn
Tajikistan is rich with cotton
Sir Darya River flows in Tajikistan.

NIGORA MAHMUDOVA, 12

* Navruz or Nowruz, traditional holiday marking the first day of spring and the traditional new year in Central Asia

Тоҷикистон бисёр зебо мебошад,
Иди Наврӯзро замин мегиранд.
Дар рӯзи ид занҳо ба сар тоқи мепӯшанд
Ба тан либоси атлас.
Дар Тоҷикистон кӯҳҳо бисёр мебошад.
Дар Тобистон ба сайру гашт мераванд
Дар Тирамоҳ пахта чини мекунанд
Тоҷикистон бо пахта бой мебошад
Дар Тоҷикистон дарёи Сир ҷорист.
Президенти Тоҷикистон Эмомалӣ
Раҳмон мебошад

Tanzania | Africa

We speak Swahili and English. • We eat rice, bananas, meat, and fruit. • We play soccer, volleyball, and netball, but we also like track-and-field events.

DAUDA RAJABU, 15

Tanzania's a nice country, a country
    well praised
It also has wealth, all of which we're proud of
If you want to believe, welcome and witness:
Tanzania's a nice country, a country
    well praised

There are animals of the jungle,
    I'll mention a few
There are those with nice faces and those
    that can't be looked at
There's the arrogant lion, giraffe,
    leopard, and others
Tanzania's a nice country, a country
    well praised

There are tall mountains that are highly praised
They have aligned themselves in rows,
    Kilimanjaro* represents them all
When you look at it you will praise it,
    and I welcome you to
Tanzania's a nice country, a country
    well praised

I will finish off here, I cannot exhaust its praises
There are too many to explain,
    welcome and witness
We don't segregate color or creed,
    Europeans or Africans
Tanzania's a nice country, a country
    well praised

Tanzania nchi nzuri, Nchi yenye kusifika,
Tena ina utajiri, Yote tuna jivunia,
Ukitaka kuamini, Karibu kushuhudia,
Tanzania nchi nzuri, Nchi yenye kusifika.

Kuna wanyama wa pori, baadhi nitatamka,
Wapo wenye sura nzuri, na wasietazamika,
Yupo simba mjeuri, twiga, chui kadharika,
Tanzania nchi nzuri, Nchi yenye kusifika.

Kuna milima mirefu, tena yenye kusifika,
Imejipanga kwa safu, Kilimanjaro yawakilisha,
Ukiitazama utajisifu, tena nakukaribisha,
Tanzania nchi nzuri, Nchi yenye kusifika.

Mimi naishiahapa, Siwezi kuyamaliza,
Yapo mengi yakuelezea, Karibu kushuhudia,
Atubagui rangi wala kabila, Wazungu na Waafrika,
Tanzania nchi nzuri, Nchi yenye kusifika.

*The highest peak in Africa at 5,892 meters, an inactive volcano in northeastern Tanzania   ARISTIDES AUDAX, 13

Thailand | Asia

We speak Thai and other tribal languages. • We eat *kao* (rice), fish, and *pad Thai* (pan-fried noodles). • We play soccer, table tennis, and badminton.

Blue sky, transparent water and beautiful wind
Has Siam*, the land of smile
Broad ocean, mountains, and forests
Peace … the land of peace thanks to his Majesty

Plenty of fish is the water,
Plenty of rice are the fields
The old people say
"Always smile and be considerate,"
These too have been in our heart since long ago.

The smile of Thailand,   Wonderful culture
Great natural resources,   Great Justice King
His well-known majesty,   His queen is always supportive
May peace be with us,   Here in Thailand, the golden land!

NIRUTCHAYA, PIYAPORN, AND YONGMEE, 12

* Ancient official name of the Kingdom of Thailand

ฟ้าสวย น้ำใส ใจงาม
คือสยามเมืองยิ้มยิ่งใหญ่
ทะเลกว้างป่าเขาเนาไพร
แผ่นดินไทยร่มเย็นพระบารมี

ในน้ำมีปลาในนามีข้าว
สุภาษิตสยามสมสมัย
ยิ้มรับขับสู้คู่น้ำใจ
วัฒนธรรมคู่ไทยมาชั่วกาล

รอยยิ้มพิมพ์สยาม   งดงามวัฒนธรรม
ชื่นฉ่ำธรรมชาติ   มหาราชทรงธรรม
เลิศล้ำพระบารมี   องค์ราชินีคู่บาท
ประชาราษฎร์ร่มเย็น   คือแผ่นดินไทยแผ่นดินทอง

KANTHISAK, KORNTHEP, JETTARIN, THANAKORN, AND SUTHASIT, 12

354

Timor-Leste | Asia

We speak Tetum and Portuguese. • We eat *modo-fila* (stir-fried vegetables), meat, and tofu. • We play soccer and basketball.

Timor … Oh Timor
The poorest country in Asia
Though you are small and poor
We will serve and bring your name forward
Among all other countries
Cause we are children
We are the future of this beloved country.

JOSE CARLOS, 12

CELESTINA XIMENES, 11

Timor... Oh Timor
rai nebe kiak liu iha ASIA
Maske o kiik no kiak
Ami sei taue o no fotio nia narau
Iha Nasaun hotu-hotu
Tamba ami mak Labarik
Futuro ba rai doben ida ne'e

Togo | Africa

We speak many languages, but our official language is French.   •   We eat corn, yams, rice, okra, and tropical fruits.   •   We play soccer and basketball.

Gombo* Sauce, Gooey Sauce

Sauce adored by the children of Togo
You whom Mother makes often,
We love you most of all
When you are accompanied by agbelim akoume**
You are swallowed with lots of meatballs
We love you, we adore you
Whether you are clear, red with little smoked fish, or dry,
We love you, we adore you
Mother, let us eat well with gombo sauce.

AKOSSIWA STELLA, 9

* Green tropical vegetable with a gooey consistency
** Maize porridge

Sauce du gombo, Sauce gluante.
Sauce adorée des enfants du Togo
Toi que maman prépare souvent.
Nous t'aimons surtout quand tu es
accompagnée de tgbelim akoumé.
Toi qui fais avaler plusieurs boullettes
de pâte. Nous t'aimons, nous t'adorons
que tu sois claire, rouge avec de
petit poissons fumés ou séchés, Nous
t'aimons, nous t'adorons. Maman
fais nous bien manger surtout avec
la Sauce du gombo

SESHIE MAWUKO, 11

Tonga | Oceania

We speak Tongan and English. • We eat yams, taro leaves, cassava, fish, and roasted pig. • We play rugby, cricket, volleyball, basketball, and tennis.

MARGARET UATA, 12

The Tauolonga (Traditional Dance)

The song of our island
Drifting in the air
The young, fine women
Let down their hair
Finally the music starts
And brings the joy into our hearts

The elegant movement
Of their hands
And costumes made
From coconut strands
With these the women
Put on a show
That will lift the spirits
Of our souls

TAINA PULOKA, 12

The Tauólunga (Traditional Dance)

The song of our island
Dripting in the air
The young, fine women
Let down their hair
Finnaly the music starts
And brings the joy into our hearts.

The elegant movement
Of their hands
And costumes made
From coconut strands.
With these the women
Puten a show
That will lift the spirits
Of our souls

Trinidad & Tobago | Central America

We speak English. • We eat chicken, baked macaroni, saltfish, rice, curried meat, and vegetables. • We play cricket, basketball, and water sports.

KRISTEN HANNYWELL, 9

Our Country T&T

Our cultures large and small
From Chinese to Indian we love them all
From Parangi* to reggae
They're all there to stay

All of our festivals from Divali** to Eid***
They are what we need
It all started when the Spaniards came
And then started our panyard's**** name

The Arawaks***** were warlike don't you see
The Caribs were peaceful and settled the sea
Carnival is full of creativity
Chinese arrival is to stay for eternity

God has blessed these blessed lands
The sunlit beaches are full of bands
Toro is where people go loco
The energy high and laziness low

So that's our island
Our historic land
The beauty of the hibiscus
And don't forget the big bus

GABRIEL VIEIRA, 9

* Type of music with Caribbean and Latin American cultural influences
** Festival of Lights, Hindu religious celebration
*** Muslim religious celebration
**** Home base of a steel band, where they practice and store their pans
***** People who were living in the West Indies

362

Tunisia | Africa

We speak Arabic and French. • We eat couscous with vegetables and meats, fish, and a wide variety of fruits. • We play soccer.

تونسَ هي بلدي... حسن بلد هي تونسَ.
نغني في المدرسة نشيد نشيدك عن تونسَ.
تونسَ هي حياتي و بلادي نا اعيش فيها كل عمري.
انا أحبُ تونسَ الخضراء، علم بلادي لونهُ أحمرُ
تتوسطهُ يدا لقمرٌ ببحثنا أ... نجمة كوفلسة.
لأن تونسَ، خير، عندك Jaime beaucoup Tunisie
و جمل خابة هي حياتي.
علم تونسَ بيوكبه به هلالٌ نجمة جميلٌ لونهُ أحمرٌ وأبيض

HAYTHEM TABOUBI, 11

Tunisia is my country, the best country is Tunisia.
At school, we sing a poem on Tunisia.
Tunisia is my life and my country; I've lived there my whole life
I like green Tunisia, the flag's color is red, with a white circle, and a star.
I like Tunisia a lot.
Because Tunisia is the best thing in my life.
The flag of Tunisia has a crescent and a beautiful star,
Its color is red and white.

NESRINE AMIRI, 12

Turkey | Eurasia

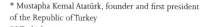

We speak Turkish and Arabic.　•　We eat lamb and rice, stuffed grape leaves, and shish kebabs.　•　We play basketball, volleyball, and soccer.

Turkey For Me

Turkey for me,
Means children and
Flowers that blossom
In the fields.

Turkey for me,
Means a tree which
Comes into flower in spring
And loses its leaves in autumn.

Turkey for me,
Means an epic
Written in history
With golden letters.

Turkey for me,
Means a big family
With Atatürk* and Aşik Veysel **
Orhan Veli** and all the people living in Anatolia.

MERVE ÖZDIL, 10

* Mustapha Kemal Atatürk, founder and first president
of the Republic of Turkey
**Turkish poets

SENA OLGUN, 10

BENiM iÇiN TÜRKiYE

Benim için TÜRKiYE
Çocuk demektir
Kırlarda açan
Çiçek demektir

Benim için TÜRKiYE
İlkbaharda tomurcuk veren
Sonbaharda yapraklarını döken
Bir ağaç demektir.

Benim için TÜRKiYE
Tarihe adını
Altın harflerle kazıyan
Bir destan demektir.

Benim için TÜRKiYE
ATATÜRK·üyle, Aşık veysel·iyle
Orhan veli·siyle, Anadoluda yaşayan insanıyla
Kostocoman bir AiLE demektir.

Turkmenistan | Asia

We speak Turkmen and Russian. • We eat a lot of meat and *chorek* (traditional Turkmen bread). • We play soccer, but we also like martial arts.

My Fatherland

To praise the fame of my country
You gave me paper and pen
Your sunny days
Encourage me my land

I listen to the birds in the morning
My country will become affluent
You are the land of Turkmen nation
Changes from day to day

Your summers are real summers and your
autumns are real autumns
I don't have enough words to praise you
If there are any nice things in this world
My land has all beauties of the world.

My grey-bearded grandpas are proud of you
And grey-haired grannies are proud of you
We are glad that our land is becoming better
You are my soul and life

MAKSAT PENDIYEW, 11

FUSYIPEWA LAGYN, 13

368

Tuvalu | Oceania

We speak Tuvaluan and English.   •   We eat spinach, fish, and tropical fruits.   •   We play soccer, basketball, touch rugby, and *kilikiti* (Samoan cricket).

EMILY KAPUAFE, 10

Tuvalu has many coconut trees
And plants to eat and drink
Tuvalu also has a nice place
And it has nine small islands
Tuvaluan people can make salad.
Tuvalu smells fresh in the morning
Tuvalu too has lots of things to use.
Tuvalu has many fish
People of Tuvalu they laugh
And tell interesting stories
Tuvalu islands are very peaceful
And kind and care and love
Tuvalu has no mountains like other islands
And people of Tuvalu drink coconut
I love Tuvalu because it's nice to go and have a picnic.

TAU PENEHURO, 10

Tuvalu has many coconut tree,
and Plants to eat and drink.
Tuvalu also have a nice place
and it has nine small Island
Tuvaluan people's can make
salad. Tuvalu smells fresh in
the morning. Tuvalu too has
lots of kind of things to use.
Tuvalu has many fish. People
of Tuvalu they laugh and
tell interesting stories. Tuvalu
Island's is very peaceful.
and kind and care and love.
Tuvalu has no mountain
like other Islands. And people
of. Tuvalu drink coconut.
I love Tuvalu because
it's nice to go and have
a picnic.

Uganda | Africa

We speak many languages, but our official language is English. • We eat eggs, meat stew, rice, peanut stew, and citrus fruits. • We play soccer.

KIYINGI AKISAM, 12

Uganda, Uganda, Uganda
The land of freedom
Full of beautiful tribes
Uganda, Uganda, Uganda
A country with wide activities

Uganda, Uganda, Uganda
Blessed with a good nature
Full of tourist attractions
Uganda, Uganda, Uganda
A beautiful country with good soils
A country with a variety of crops

Uganda, Uganda, Uganda
The peace of Africa
A country full of flowing rivers
A country full of beautiful animals
Oh! Uganda
I pray to bless you forever.

MUSA SULTAN, 12

Ukraine | Europe

We speak Ukrainian and Russian. • We eat sausages, *salo* (pork fat), corn, soup, and crepes. • We play soccer, basketball, volleyball, and ice hockey.

Соловʼїні далі, далі солові̇ні...

Соловʼїні далі, далі солові̇ні
знов весна розквітла на мо̇ій Вкраїні
На гіллі рясному цвіт немов сніжинки,
Знову серце бʼється молодо і дзвінко...
Я їду до гаю. краю, ти мій краю,
Кращого за тебе я в тишині не знаю!
Кращого не знаю далі мої сини,
Як весну стрічаєш на Вкраїні милій!
У росі фіалки, ріки у тумані...
в серці сяють очі, сині і кохані...
В пташинім щебеті все кругом проснулось,
У до мене знову молодість вернулась.
Я їду до гаю, і в блакить безкраю
Серце моє тихе й тихцею співає
Про весну чудесну на моїй Вкраїні...
Соловʼїні далі, далі соловʼїні!

SASHA ALEKSEEVA, 12

Nightingale Horizons, Horizons of Nightingales

Nightingale horizons, horizons of nightingales
Spring is in blossom again in my Ukraine
The blossom is so thick on the bushes, like snowflakes,
Again young hearts are beating loudly
As I go to the grove—my place, oh my place,
I don't know any better place in my life!
I don't know any better time
Than meeting spring in my beloved Ukraine,

When violets are covered with dew, the river is in fog,
When eyes sparkle, and hearts are in love,
Everything around has awoken
My youth is flourishing, too.
I go to the grove beneath the endless clouds
My heart is singing
about the wonderful spring in my Ukraine …
Nightingale horizons, horizons of nightingales.

TARAS KRAVCHENKO, 12

United Arab Emirates | Asia (Middle East)

We speak Arabic and English. • We eat rice, lamb, fish, seafood, fruit and vegetables, and *raqaq* (thin bread served with sauce). • We play soccer.

I am stuck in the U.A.E.*
I would like to see Abu Dhabi**
I am a Muslim and I like to study
Cause all I have to do
Is to make my family happy

All I see is deserts and buildings
Sands and lands
All over the place
You should see Dubai U.A.E.
Everybody is free
Cause all we have to do
Is look closely

SOPHIE, 9

* United Arab Emirates
** Capital city of the U.A.E.

Oasis

Desert Fox

TOMMY BODO, 9

I am stuck in the U.A.E

I would like to visit Abu Dhabi
I am a Muslim and I like to study
Cause all I have to do is to make
my family happy

All I see is deserts and
Buildings sands and lands all over
the place you should see Dubai U.A.E
everybody is free cause all we have
to do is look closely

376

United Kingdom | Europe

We speak English. • We eat bacon, sausages, beans, Yorkshire pudding, and meat pies. • We play soccer, tennis, cricket, and *snooker* (similar to pool).

JEREMY REES, 10

My Country!

This country is excellent
There are magnificent things to see
All the things they set up just for you and me
Lots of people who grow older
Have tons of tea!
Eating in the fish shop
With all those horrible soggy chips
Look what happens
I eat too much
I get fatty hips
England England
What a wonderful place to be

All those cinemas with popcorn
And ice cold drinks waiting for me
Exciting rides that make your belly go wee
But when you get off it you fall over
And bump your knee
England England
What a wonderful place to be
Sitting in front of TV relaxing
England England
What a wonderful place to be
Come on have some
It's waiting for you and me

FRASER, 10

My country!

This country is excellent theres magnificent things to see
All the things they set up just for you and me. In the
Lots of people growing older have tons of tea! Eating the fish
Shop with all those horrible sogy chips look what happens
when I eats to much I get fatty hips England England
what a wonderful place to be all those cinemas with pop corn
and a ice cold drink waiting for me. Exciting rides what mate
your belly go weee but when you get off if your fall over
and bump your knee. England England what a wonderful
place to be sitting in front tv relaxing.
England England what a wonderful place to be come
on have some it's waiting for you and me.

United States of America | North America

We speak English. • We eat hamburgers, french fries, pizza, chicken, and fruit and vegetables. • We play baseball, American football, and basketball.

SHARON K., 11

United States of America

America is made up of fifty states
Some are good and some are great

Some are red and some are blue,
But all of them have citizens like me and you.

We have oceans, mountains, deserts, and lakes
We survive tornadoes, hurricanes,
Thunderstorms, and earthquakes.

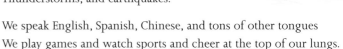

We speak English, Spanish, Chinese, and tons of other tongues
We play games and watch sports and cheer at the top of our lungs.

We elect our government,
And are free to disagree without fear of punishment.

We have freedom of religion, speech, and the press.
It's so nice to know we can always express.

I wish we weren't at war,
But I will always love my country evermore.

A.J. SMITH, 11

Uruguay | South America

We speak Spanish. • We eat *asado* (grilled beef) and fruit and vegetables. • We play soccer, basketball, volleyball, and water sports.

CARNAVAL DEL URUGUAY

Mi ermosa tierra

Las aves cantan, y comen migajas
El gaucho, sentado,
al pie de un frondoso árbol
toca melancólico su guitarra.

Al anochecer la luna asoma
la china, bonita y compañera
le alcanza sonriente el mate
y el gaucho percibe su aroma

Cantando y tocando todos los paisanos
en rueda de mate
contemplan la aurora, esperando alegres
la carne fresquita para el rico asado.

My Beautiful Land

The birds are singing and eating bread crumbs
The cowboy is sitting
To the foot of a leafy tree,
Melancholic, playing guitar

At nightfall, the moon appears
The young girl, good looking,
Smiling, hands him the mate*
And the cowboy senses its scent

Singing and playing music, all the countrymen
In the mate circle**
Admire the dawn, happily waiting
For the fresh meat to roast.

LEONARDO MARA, 10

* Mate is a herbal infusion drunk from a gourd with a straw
** The mate gourd is filled with hot water repeatedly and shared in a circular ceremony

VANESSA FRANCO DIAZ, 10

Uzbekistan | Asia

We speak Uzbek and Russian.   •   We eat rice, beef, chicken, rabbit, *manty* (dumplings), and fruit and vegetables.   •   We play soccer and basketball.

RAHMANOVA ZEBO, 10

Uzbekistan is my motherland
Apricots are yellow and orange
The weather is fine and warm
The sun is yellow.

The cotton grows
And mountains blossom
It's always warm.

Uzbeks wear national clothes
We have many friends: Kazakhs, Turkmens, and many others
That is why I wrote this poem:
There are no people in the world friendlier and kinder than here.

ABDULLAEV ARTUR, 10

Узбекистан Родина моя.
Абрикосы жёлтые оранживые.
Погода хорошая, тёплая,
Солнце жёлтое.

Здесь хлопок растёт,
И горы цветут.
Всегда здесь тепло.

Узбекистанцы носят национальную одежду
У нас много друзей. Казахстан, Туркменистан
И много других
Поэтому я сочинил этот стих.
Нет в мире людей
Дружней и добрей

Vanuatu | Oceania

We speak many languages, but mostly English and French.   •   We eat rice, yams, noodles, and vegetables.   •   We play soccer, volleyball, and netball.

This is my traditional dressing up in my home Island "Tanna" "TOKA DANCE"

Vanuatu, the Untouched Paradise

Vanuatu is one of the countries in the Pacific Islands
The islands are green as a frog
There is no war and starvation
People live peacefully,
you can hear laughter of children
And a friendly smile from people
Everywhere you go.
We claim ourselves to be Ni-Vans* with black skin
And have strong and healthy bodies
That's why we keep our tradition and culture alive.
Vanuatu, we will never give up on you
Like in our motto it says, "In God we stand."

MARIE WILLIAMS, 13

*The people of Vanuatu are known as Ni-Vanuatu or Ni-Vans

MARIE NAMAK, 13

VANUATU THE UNTOUCHED PARADISE
Vanuatu is one of the countries in the Pacific islands.
The islands are green as a frog.
There is no war and no starvation.
People live peacfully, you can hear laughter of children
and a friendly smile from people every where you go.
We clam ourselves to be Ni-Vans with black skin
and strong and healthy bodies. Thats why we
keep our tradition and culture alive.
Vanuatu we will never give up on you
like in our moto it says in God we stand.

Venezuela | South America

We speak Spanish. • We eat rice, beans, cheese, chicken, fish, corn, *arepas* (deep-fried pancake), and tropical fruits. • We play baseball and basketball.

Venezuela se encuentran cosas como las ferias.
En Venezuela se aprenden a vestirnos
Nace un país lindo donde podemos ser feliz.
Estamos feliz de nuestro país.
Zulia es de todo.

Unido podemos jugar a fútbol y bailar salsa
Encontramos muchas cosas bonitas en Venezuela, rio, lagos y el mar
Las escuelas nos enseñan cosas como a leer y escribir
Arepas me gusta comer.

In Venezuela you find things like markets
In Venezuela we learn to dress
A beautiful country is born where we can be happy
We are happy of our country
Zulia* is of everyone
Together we can play football and dance salsa
We find many nice things in Venezuela, rivers,
lakes, and the sea
The schools teach us things like reading and writing
I like to eat arepas**

ANDREA ORTEGA, 12

MARY EVELYN BARROSO, 12

* Estado Zulia is one of Venezuela's twenty-three states
** Small pancake-shape bread made with corn flour

Vietnam | Asia

We speak Vietnamese. • We eat white rice, *nuoc mam* (fish sauce), boiled vegetables, and fruit. • We play volleyball, soccer, badminton, and tennis.

NGUYEN AI Q NHU, 12

My Country

My country has rows of green coconut trees
And golden paddy fields
During summer afternoons
From the distance
Flocks of storks are landing down to the fields

My country has large rivers
The tide goes up and down daily
Boats crossing everywhere
In the morning and afternoon too

I love my country
With the shade of the green coconut tree
With the hovering storks
And golden paddy fields*

KIM PHUONG, 9

* Flooded parcel of land used for growing rice

Yemen

Asia (Middle East)

We speak Arabic. • We eat soup, fish, chicken, goat, beef, rice, bread, beans, egg pancakes, boiled potatoes, and meat sandwiches. • We play soccer.

FATIMA AHMED, 13

Today I feel proud and I call / My country the glory of the nations
I give her my blood and my heart / And I protect the symbol of my country
My nation, country of peace / My nation, protected by God

You are the sun / And we are the moon
You are the moon / And we are the stars
You are the pen / And we are the handbook
You are the school / And we are the students

You are the Happy Yemen

EMAN ABADO, 11

اليمن

الاسم ايمان عبده محمد الشامي
العمر: ١١ سنه
اليوم افخر واقادي   وطني يا وطنا الامجاد
افديك بالروحي وفؤادي واصونك رمز لبلادي
و لمتي يا وطني السلام   وطني طامولنا يرعاك
قد عادت يعز مولانا   فخري و دمي مسرك
✳ ✳
انتي الشمس   وما حنا القمر
انتي الا قمر   وناحنا النجوم
انتي المعلم   ونحن الدفتر
انتي المدرسه   ونحن الطالب

انتي اليمن السعيده

Zambia | Africa

We speak many different languages, but mostly English. • We eat *nsima* (cornmeal), soups, and vegetables. • We play soccer and netball.

STUDENTS OF AISHA PROJECT SCHOOL, 9

This is a ball
I like to kick the ball in Zambia
Zambia is green
I like to swim in the river
The river is blue
The elephant is big and grey
I like to have chicken in my stomach
I give rice to two brothers and three sisters
I like to play with them in the blue river
I'm smiling—I'm happy
This is my life in Zambia

STEVEN MUIEGA, 12

This Is a Balls
I LIFE kick the BolliN ZAMBIA
ZAMBIA IS gReEN
I LIKE to suuinN the river
the riverisbLuE
the ELEPhaNtis big and gray
I LIKE CHICKEN IN MY StomicH
I give rice to two brothers and three SisteI
I LIKE to PLAYwWithELE m IN river bLUE
Im smiling - Im Happy
This is my LIFE IN ZAMBIA

394

Zimbabwe | Africa

We speak English, Shona, and Ndebele. • We eat *sadza* (porridge), vegetables, meat, insects, and tropical fruits. • We play soccer and basketball.

Zimbabwe is Beautiful

In rural areas
There is no rain
People go to caves
To cook beer
To please the ancestors and ask for rain
When the beer evaporates, people are happy
Ancestors have drunk, and they can revive rain!

In Zimbabwe there are caves,
Rivers, buildings, and animals

People in Zimbabwe have a good culture
They go to church with a heart
And children go to school

Many years ago there were no telephones
People beat drums, and used fire and wood
When smoke rose up, people knew
Something wrong had happened and came to help

BRIGHTON CHOVUNITA, 12

giraffe

bull

house

Father

house

Sister

mother

children

dance

hen

dog

SYNODIA, 12

Zimbabwe is Beautiful
In rural areas
There is no rain
people go to cave
To cook beer
to please The ancestors and ask for rain
when the beer evaporates people are happy
Ancestor have drank and they can reive rain

In Zimbabwe there are caves
rivers building and animals

people in zimbabwe have a good caulture
They go to church whith a Heart
and children go to school

many years ogo there were no telephones
People beat drums and used faire and wood
when simoke rose up people knew
some thing wrong heppened and came to help

Country Statistics and Credits

AFGHANISTAN
Primary school enrollment: 53%
Population under 18: 54%
Total population: 27,145,000
Drawing: Fatah Mohammad, grade 6
Poetry: Nazila Gran, grade 4
Schools: Fatima Balki Girls' High School & Atta Mohammad Noor Boys High School
Translator: Ahmad Seiar Razaie
Original text: Dari

ALBANIA
Primary school enrollment: 52%
Population under 18: 31%
Total population: 3,190,000
Drawing: Armando Bektashi, grade 5
Poetry: Arlinda Sela, grade 6
Schools: Shkolla "Naim Fraskeri" & SOS Children's Village
Translator: SOS Children's Village
Original text: Albanese

ALGERIA
Primary school enrollment: 97%
Population under 18: 35%
Total population: 33,858,000
Drawing: Haoua Hardi, grade 5
Poetry: Meliha Mehdi, grade 5
School: El Rafik School
Translator: Catherine Kennedy
Original text: French

ANDORRA
Primary school enrollment: 89%
Population under 18: 19%
Total population: 75,000
Drawing: Carla & Andrea, grade 4
Poetry: Matthew Robinson, grade 4
School: École Française
Translator: Rebecca Gibergues
Original text: French

ANGOLA
Primary school enrollment: 58%
Population under 18: 53%
Total population: 15,941,000
Drawing: Validna Manuel, grade 4
Poetry: Dinamene Calete, grade 4
School: Escola Primaria n. 2004
Translator: Joana Santos
Original text: Portuguese

ANTIGUA & BARBUDA
Primary school enrollment: data not available
Population under 18: 33%
Total population: 85,000
Drawing: Keiann & Ashmanie, grade 4
Poetry: Joseph Kwamayne, grade 4
School: T. N. Kirnon School
Original text: English

ARGENTINA
Primary school enrollment: 99%
Population under 18: 32%
Total population: 38,747,000
Drawing: Milena Casco & Lucas Degregorio, grade 4
Poetry: Andrea Liliana Rojo, grade 4
School: Escuela Primaria nb. 33 Resistencia
Translator: Stéphanie Rabemiafara
Original text: Spanish

ARMENIA
Primary school enrollment: 94%
Population under 18: 25%
Total population: 3,002,000
Drawing: Emma Gardilian, grade 5
Poetry: Liana Harutunyan, grade 5
School: H. Hayrapetyan School nb. 78
Translator: Mariam Sukhudyan
Original text: Armenian

AUSTRALIA
Primary school enrollment: 96%
Population under 18: 24%
Total population: 20,155,000
Drawing: Jaala, grade 6
Poetry: Fletcher Horne, grade 6
School: Manly Primary School
Original text: English

AUSTRIA
Primary school enrollment: data not available
Population under 18: 19%
Total population: 8,189,000
Drawing: Laura Franz, grade 3
Poetry: Carolin, grade 3
School: Volksschule Mauer VS I
Translator: Marcia Martinez
Original text: German

AZERBAIJAN
Primary school enrollment: 91%
Population under 18: 30%
Total population: 8,467,000
Drawing: Mamisova, grade 7
Poetry: Bagirova Nilufar, grade 5
School: Lyceum 220
Translator: Yvette Haker
Original text: Azeri

BAHAMAS
Primary school enrollment: 84%
Population under 18: 32%
Total population: 331,000
Drawing: Keshone Morley, grade 3
Poetry: Jada Sweeting, grade 3
Schools: Mt. Carmel Preparatory Academy & Queen's College
Original text: English

BAHRAIN
Primary school enrollment: 86%
Population under 18: 30%
Total population: 753,000
Drawing: Fatima Jassin Ridha, grade 5
Poetry: Anfal Hussain, grade 6
School: Arabian Pearl Gulf School
Original text: English

BANGLADESH
Primary school enrollment: 84%
Population under 18: 42%
Total population: 141,822,000
Drawing: Fatima Khatun Tamin, grade 4
Poetry: Rocky Bul, grade 4
School: Baliadanga Model, Government Primary School
Translator: Shantona Momtaz
Original text: Bangla

BARBADOS
Primary school enrollment: 97%
Population under 18: 23%
Total population: 270,000
Drawing: Aaron Hewitt, grade 4
Poetry: Kendra Bovell, grade 4
School: Hillaby Turner's Hall Primary School
Original text: English

BELARUS
Primary school enrollment: 90%
Population under 18: 20%
Total population: 9,755,000
Drawing: Liza Linchenko, grade 3
Poetry: M. Tremvekova, grade 5
School: School nb.136 Minsk
Translator: Natasha V.
Original text: Belarussian

BELGIUM
Primary school enrollment: 99%
Population under 18: 20%
Total population: 10,419,000
Drawing: Marjan Suffys, Kelsey Depuydt, grade 6
Poetry: Hayley Rollez, grade 6
School: De Tweesprong
Translator: Anthony Asael
Original text: Dutch

BELIZE
Primary school enrollment: 95%
Population under 18: 43%
Total population: 288,000
Drawing: Henry Figueroa, grade 4
Poetry: Eric Ruano, grade 4
School: El Progreso Government School
Translator: Stéphanie Rabemiafara
Original text: Spanish

BENIN
Primary school enrollment: 54%
Population under 18: 51%
Total population: 8,439,000
Drawing: Gbenouvonon Florent, grade 5
Poetry: Nouatin Sabine, grade 4
School: Kode Public Primary School
Translator: Stéphanie Bourassa
Original text: French

BHUTAN
Primary school enrollment: 70%
Population under 18: 45%
Total population: 2,163,000
Drawing: Yeshi Dema, grade 4
Poetry: Sauharan Thatipamula Nenkata, grade 4
School: Sunshine School
Original text: English

BOLIVIA
Primary school enrollment: 78%
Population under 18: 44%
Total population: 9,525,000
Drawing: Liset Mamani Romero, grade 5
Poetry: German Portugal Cuevas, grade 8
School: Escuela Union Europea
Translator: José Miguel Neira
Original text: Spanish

BOSNIA & HERZEGOVINA
Primary school enrollment: 93%
Population under 18: 21%
Total population: 3,907,000
Drawing: Anel Gradascenic, grade 6
Poetry: Adna Arslanovic, grade 4
School: JU OS Dzemaludin Causevic
Translator: Ewa Golijanin
Original text: Bosnian

BOTSWANA
Primary school enrollment: 82%
Population under 18: 45%
Total population: 1,765,000
Drawing: Chipo Hamaluba, grade 3
Poetry: Patience Pilane, grade 6
School: Raserura Primary School
Original text: English

BRAZIL
Primary school enrollment: 96%
Population under 18: 33%
Total population: 186,405,000
Drawing: Ana Dias Goes, grade 4
Poetry: Bianca da Silva Aroyo Zaraty, grade 4
Schools: Etnia Hupd'äh dos povos indígenas do Alto Rio Negro-Am - Aldeia - Yuyu Dëh & State School Castro Alves
Translator: Stéphanie Rabemiafara
Original text: Portuguese

BRUNEI
Primary school enrollment: data not available
Population under 18: 35%
Total population: 374,000
Drawing: Khairiah Hafizah Binti & Abdel Aziz, grade 4
Poetry: Abdel Hadi, grade 4
School: Bakti Dewa School
Translator: Teachers of Bakti Dewa School
Original text: Malay

BULGARIA
Primary school enrollment: 95%
Population under 18: 18%
Total population: 7,726,000
Drawing: Neli, grade 1
Poetry: Lora, grade 5
School: SOS Children's Village
Translator: Savina Bogoeva
Original text: Bulgarian

BURKINA FASO
Primary school enrollment: 32%
Population under 18: 54%
Total population: 13,228,000
Drawing: Various students, grade 2
Poetry: Safiatou, Naab, & Bourima, grade 2
School: Association Espoir pour Demain
Translator: Sophie Walenda
Original text: French & Dioula

BURUNDI
Primary school enrollment: 47%
Population under 18: 53%
Total population: 7,548,000
Drawing: Quintia Iradukunda, grade 5
Poetry: Béni Muhizi, grade 5
School: Ecole Internationale de Bujumbura
Translator: Stéphanie Rabemiafara
Original text: French

CAMBODIA
Primary school enrollment: 65%
Population under 18: 44%
Total population: 14,071,000
Drawing: Chin Vida, grade 5
Poetry: Prorn Thavith, grade 6
School: Hermann Gmeiner School
Translator: Hermann Gmeiner School
Original text: Khmer

CAMEROON
Primary school enrollment: 79%
Population under 18: 48%
Total population: 16,322,000
Drawing: Maira Mouboubou, grade 5
Poetry: Clarisse, grade 5
School: Harde Primary School
Translator: Ghalia Hachem
Original text: French

CANADA
Primary school enrollment: 99%
Population under 18: 21%
Total population: 32,876,000
Drawing: Autumn French, grade 5
Poetry: Krystal Cabico, grade 5
School: Our Lady of Lourdes Catholic School
Original text: English

CAPE VERDE
Primary school enrollment: 92%
Population under 18: 47%
Total population: 507,000
Drawing: Premise, grade 4
Poetry: Ana Paula, grade 4
School: Escola Lavadouro
Translator: Stéphanie Rabemiafara
Original text: Portuguese

CENTRAL AFRICAN REPUBLIC
Primary school enrollment: 43%
Population under 18: 50%
Total population: 4,038,000
Drawing: Gboutet Arielle, grade 5
Poetry: Bado Irenee, grade 5
School: Ngaragba Mixt School
Translator: Stéphanie Rabemiafara
Original text: French

CHAD
Primary school enrollment: 36%
Population under 18: 54%
Total population: 9,749,000
Drawing: Mahamat Idriss, grade 4
Poetry: Adam Abdoulaye, Kelou Bourdamsou & Adam Abanour, grade 4
School: Ecole nomade de Mani Kossam
Translator: School teachers
Original text: Peul & Arabic

CHILE
Primary school enrollment: data not available
Population under 18: 30%
Total population: 16,295,000
Drawing: Evelyn Delgado, grade 7
Poetry: María Santana Lleufu, grade 5
School: Fundación mi Casa
Translator: Claudia Serey
Original text: Spanish

CHINA
Primary school enrollment: 99%
Population under 18: 27%
Total population: 1,315,844,000
Drawing: Liu Hongying, grade 4
Poetry: Li Yuanyuan, grade 4
School: Da Xing Chang Primary School
Translator: Sinba Duan
Original text: Mandarin

COLOMBIA
Primary school enrollment: 91%
Population under 18: 35%
Total population: 46,156,000
Drawing: David Aguirre, grade 5
Poetry: Ximena Godoy Menidivil, grade 3
School: Escuela Primaria de Tierrabomba
Translator: Katia Vandeputte
Original text: Spanish

COMOROS
Primary school enrollment: 31%
Population under 18: 48%
Total population: 839,000
Drawing: Lamyat Bacar, grade 5
Poetry: Nouraynat Hassan, grade 5
School: Abdoulhamid School
Translator: Catherine Kennedy
Original text: French

CONGO (DEMOCRATIC REPUBLIC)
Primary school enrollment: 52%
Population under 18: 54%
Total population: 57,549,000
Drawing: Kambala Ornella, grade 5
Poetry: Mulumba Jemimah, grade 5
School: Primary School Mfamial Le
Bambino
Translator: Richard Higgs
Original text: French

CONGO (REPUBLIC)
Primary school enrollment: data not
available
Population under 18: 54%
Total population: 3,999,000
Drawing: Nkenda Baloki, grade 4
Poetry: Kinkela Jolda, grade 4
Schools: Ecole des Trois Francs &
Ecole Notre Dame
Translator: Richard Higgs
Original text: French

COSTA RICA
Primary school enrollment: data not
available
Population under 18: 33%
Total population: 4,468,000
Drawing: Sebastian Hidalgo Vargas,
grade 4
Poetry: Chrystell Viquez Campos,
grade 6
School: Escuela Marisa
Translator: Jakob Hans Renpening
Original text: Spanish

COTE D'IVOIRE
Primary school enrollment: 56%
Population under 18: 49%
Total population: 18,154,000
Drawing: Nabagate Barakissa,
grade 4
Poetry: Toure Ibrahim, grade 4
School: Circonscription Scolaire
d'Anyama
Translator: Paulina
Original text: French

CROATIA
Primary school enrollment: 87%
Population under 18: 19%
Total population: 4,551,000
Drawing: Kathrina Stancic, grade 4
Poetry: Iva Hodak, grade 4
School: O.S. Ivan Merz
Translator: Krešimir Hrdlicka
Original text: Croatian

CUBA
Primary school enrollment: 96%
Population under 18: 24%
Total population: 11,269,000
Drawing: Ángel Luis & Elvis López,
grade 4
Poetry: Flavia Perez, grade 4
School: Escuela Adela Azary
Labrador
Translator: Agustina Dillon
Original text: Spanish

CYPRUS
Primary school enrollment: 96%
Population under 18: 25%
Total population: 835,000
Drawing: Hercules Pelivanides
grade 6
Poetry: Erineos Agathaggelou,
grade 6
School: 3rd School of Palouriotissa
Translator: Noni Hadjinikolaou
Original text: Greek

CZECH REPUBLIC
Primary school enrollment: data not
available
Population under 18: 18%
Total population: 10,220,000
Drawing: Veronika Taborikova,
grade 4
Poetry: Petr Kratochvi & Jan
Vastechovsky, grade 4
School: ZS Fr. Plaminkove
Translator: Jana Reznickova
Original text: Czech

DENMARK
Primary school enrollment: 100%
Population under 18: 22%
Total population: 5,442,000
Drawing: Thea Fisker, grade 3
Poetry: Sukaena Aktam, grade 3
School: Hillerødgades Skole
Translator: Mette Walsted
Original text: Danish

DJIBOUTI
Primary school enrollment: 33%
Population under 18: 44%
Total population: 833,000
Drawing: Houda Mohamed Hassan,
grade 4
Poetry: Marwa Ahmed Hagui, grade 4
School: École Primaire d'Engueilla
Translators: Patricia Quirk & Karla
de Greef
Original text: French

DOMINICA
Primary school enrollment: 88%
Population under 18: 34%
Total population: 79,000
Drawing: Sherlin Baron, grade 3
Poetry: Shaheeda Henderson, grade 4
School: Grand Bay Primary School &
Saint Lukes Primary School
Original text: English

DOMINICAN REPUBLIC
Primary school enrollment: 86%
Population under 18: 39%
Total population: 9,760,000
Drawing: Jomaira Velasquez Mateo,
grade 8
Poetry: Maria Yessenia Perez
Saldana, grade 8
School: Los Praditos
Translator: Rebecca Monge
Original text: Spanish

ECUADOR
Primary school enrollment: 98%
Population under 18: 39%
Total population: 13,228,000
Drawing: Analy Pavón, grade 5
Poetry: Guillermo Changún, grade 4
School: SOS Children's Villages Ibarra
Translator: Elizabeth Chatfield
Original text: Spanish

EGYPT
Primary school enrollment: 83%
Population under 18: 40%
Total population: 74,033,000
Drawing: Various students, grade 4
Poetry: Mohamed Bekhit Abou El
Fadl, grade 6
School: Al Talee Beenagee Khayreya
School
Translator: Aisha Abbasi
Original text: Arabic

EL SALVADOR
Primary school enrollment: 92%
Population under 18: 39%
Total population: 6,857,000
Drawing: Alisson Gomez Nieto,
grade 5
Poetry: Jorge Ernesto Granados,
grade 5
School: Colegio Federal Juan
Ramon Bellozo
Translator: Jenny Jonson
Original text: Spanish

EQUATORIAL GUINEA
Primary school enrollment: 61%
Population under 18: 51%
Total population: 504,000
Drawing: Jacinta Ngono Nguema,
grade 6
Poetry: Maria del Rosario Mangue
Ebendeng Ocono, grade 6
Schools: Carmen Sales Primary
School & Enrique Nvo Oke Nve
Primary School
Translator: Richard Higgs
Original text: Spanish

ERITREA
Primary school enrollment: 67%
Population under 18: 50%
Total population: 4,851,000
Drawing: Bana Mussie, grade 5
Poetry: Soliana Tekeste, grade 4
School: Sembel Primary School
Translator: Awet Araya Bahlbi
Original text: Tigrinya

ESTONIA
Primary school enrollment: 94%
Population under 18: 20%
Total population: 1,330,000
Drawing: Taavi Meinberg, grade 3
Poetry: Margo Rodi & Tanel Kiisla, grade 3
School: Tallinn Laagna Kindergarten & Basic School
Translator: Kerttu
Original text: Estonian

ETHIOPIA
Primary school enrollment: 31%
Population under 18: 51%
Total population: 83,099,000
Drawing: Eden Kebede, grade 5
Poetry: Bezawit Workeye & Rakeb Megbar, grade 5
School: Dandi Borum School
Translators: Bezawit Workeye & Rakeb Megbar
Original text: Amharic

FIJI
Primary school enrollment: 96%
Population under 18: 37%
Total population: 848,000
Drawing: Michelle Lee, grade 7
Poetry: Polly Vatu, grade 7
School: Nadi Airport School
Original text: English

FINLAND
Primary school enrollment: 99%
Population under 18: 21%
Total population: 5,249,000
Drawing: Funny Saturday Children
Poetry: Funny Saturday Children
School: Pääkaupunkiseudun Omaishoitajat ja Läheiset ry
Translator: Jonna Kilkki
Original text: Finnish

FRANCE
Primary school enrollment: 99%
Population under 18: 22%
Total population: 61,647,000
Drawing: Radouane, grade 5
Poetry: Matthieu Doré, grade 3
School: Victor Hugo
Translator: Alisha Reaves
Original text: French

GABON
Primary school enrollment: 94%
Population under 18: 47%
Total population: 1,384,000
Drawing: Pouabou Junior, grade 5
Poetry: Mihindou Clevis, grade 5
Schools: Alenakiri-Owendo, Ozoungue, Mindoube, Akournam I (Owendo); F.O.P.I, Akournam II, Owendo Octra II, Batavea, & Damas I
Translator: Richard Higgs
Original text: French

GAMBIA
Primary school enrollment: 53%
Population under 18: 46%
Total population: 1,517,000
Drawing: Gideon Abraham, grade 4
Poetry: Gideon Abraham, grade 4
School: Amazing Grace School
Original text: English

GEORGIA
Primary school enrollment: 93%
Population under 18: 23%
Total population: 4,395,000
Drawing: Iamze Mchedluri & Luda Chilachava, grade 4
Poetry: Eva Shekriladze, grade 4
School: SOS Children's Village Tbilissi
Translator: The school
Original text: Georgian

GERMANY
Primary school enrollment: data not available
Population under 18: 18%
Total population: 82,689,000
Drawing: Serdal Aydin, grade 5
Poetry: Serdal Aydin, grade 5
School: Eugen-Langen-Schule
Translator: Marcia Martinez
Original text: German

GHANA
Primary school enrollment: 65%
Population under 18: 46%
Total population: 22,113,000
Drawing: Christina Acquah, grade 5
Poetry: Elizabeth Andoh, grade 5
School: Jacob Wilson Sey Primary School
Original text: English

GREECE
Primary school enrollment: 99%
Population under 18: 17%
Total population: 11,120,000
Drawing: Fotini Papaleonidopoulou, grade 6
Poetry: Elen Labroboulou, grade 5
School: SOS Children's Village Vari
Translator: George S.
Original text: Greek

GRENADA
Primary school enrollment: 84%
Population under 18: 40%
Total population: 106,000
Drawing: Ronnie Ross, grade 6
Poetry: Adreene Forsyth, grade 6
School: The Kids Learning Centre
Original text: English

GUATEMALA
Primary school enrollment: 93%
Population under 18: 49%
Total population: 13,354,000
Drawing: Catarina Lux Us, grade 4
Poetry: Ana Tum Lopez, grade 6
School: Escuela Oficial Rural Mixta de Xegüinacabaj
Translator: Alix Quan
Original text: K'iche

GUINEA BISSAU
Primary school enrollment: 39%
Population under 18: 54%
Total population: 1,586,000
Drawing: Joana Djalo Ribeiro Santiago, grade 4
Poetry: Tiago Costa, grade 4
School: Associacao da Escola Portuguesa
Translator: Stéphanie Rabemiafara
Original text: Portuguese

GUINEA
Primary school enrollment: 57%
Population under 18: 50%
Total population: 9,402,000
Drawing: Various students, grade 4
Poetry: Mahawa Conde, grade 4
School: Ecole Sainte Marie
Translator: Livia Ferolla
Original text: French

GUYANA
Primary school enrollment: 97%
Population under 18: 35%
Total population: 751,000
Drawing: Dianna & Sofroh Hosea, grade 3
Poetry: Helena Lyte & Ray McWatt, grade 3
School: Bartica Primary School
Original text: English

HAITI
Primary school enrollment: 55%
Population under 18: 44%
Total population: 9,598,000
Drawing: Jonas Marcelus, grade 4
Poetry: Pierre Bréchel Chéry, grade 6
Schools: Collège de Côte Plage & Foyer Culturel St. Vincent de Paul
Translator: Fondation Culture Création
Original text: Créole

HONDURAS
Primary school enrollment: 91%
Population under 18: 46%
Total population: 7,106,000
Drawing : Patrick Miguel M., grade 6
Poetry: Karla Patricia, grade 6
School: Escuela Católica Santa Maria Goretti
Translators : Agustina Dillon & Janina Ralda
Original text: Spanish

HUNGARY
Primary school enrollment: 89%
Population under 18: 19%
Total population: 10,098,000
Drawing: Andrási Szilvia, grade 3
Poetry: Hannah Malaika Galambas, Anna Kubitsch, Alex Papp, grade 3
School: Laude Javne School
Translator: Katalin Dobrovotzky
Original text: Hungarian

ICELAND
Primary school enrollment: 99%
Population under 18: 26%
Total population: 301,000
Drawing: Ingi Gudmundsson, grade 6
Poetry: Pordis Olof Sigurjonsdottir, grade 6
School: Granda Primary School
Translator: Birna Juliusdottir
Original text: Icelandic

INDIA
Primary school enrollment: 76%
Population under 18: 38%
Total population: 1,169,016,000
Drawing: Sammat Manju Hansa, grade 7
Poetry: Shinika & Balikay, grade 7
School: Girls´Rural Education Center
Translator: Sonal Jalan
Original text: Hindi

INDONESIA
Primary school enrollment: 94%
Population under 18: 34%
Total population: 222,781,000
Drawing: Rizka M., grade 3
Poetry: Dewi Sviistia, grade 3
School: Dahlia Elementary School
Translator: Jean-Baptiste & Erika Rosset
Original text: Indonesian

IRAN
Primary school enrollment: data not available
Population under 18: 29%
Total population: 64,233,000
Drawing: Kimia Assadian, grade 4
Poetry: Helia Kavoosi, grade 5
School: Shahid Mahdavi
Translator: Helia Kavoosi
Original text: Farsi

IRAQ
Primary school enrollment: 78%
Population under 18: 48%
Total population: 28,993,000
Drawing: Alind Sherzad, grade 5
Poetry: Ayia Amir Ismael, grade 5
School: Zewa Center
Translator: Saleem Sadeeq Haji Al Zebari
Original text: Kurdish

IRELAND
Primary school enrollment: 96%
Population under 18: 24%
Total population: 4,148,000
Drawing: Cian McLoughlin, grade 6
Poetry: Jack Farell, grade 6
School: Griffith Barracks School
Original text: English

ISRAEL
Primary school enrollment: 98%
Population under 18: 33%
Total population: 6,725,000
Drawing: Various students, grade 3
Poetry: Ori, grade 3
School: Netanya Democratic School
Translator: Jonathan Howard
Original text: Hebrew

ITALY
Primary school enrollment: 99%
Population under 18: 17%
Total population: 58,093,000
Drawing: Deborah Sebastiani,
grade 4
Poetry: Laura Mastelotto, grade 4
School: Instituto Omero, Scuola
Giulio Romano
Translator: Elisa Capuano
Original text: Italian

JAMAICA
Primary school enrollment: 91%
Population under 18: 37%
Total population: 2,714,000
Drawing: Shirley, grade 3
Poetry: Shaquilla, grade 3
School: Allman Primary School
Original text: English

JAPAN
Primary school enrollment: 100%
Population under 18: 17%
Total population: 128,085,000
Drawing: Watabe Shun, grade 2
Poetry: Mai Sugie, Reira Morita,
Yuuka Hijikata, Ryota Hiramatsu,
grade 2
School: Kamishimada Primary
School
Translator: Yurika Mochizuki
Original text: Japanese

JORDAN
Primary school enrollment: 99%
Population under 18: 43%
Total population: 5,703,000
Drawing: Ahmad Tayseer, grade 6
Poetry: Nahla Al-Jittan, grade 4
School: Al Bayan School
Translator: Rula Abdel Hamid
Original text: Arabic

KAZAKHSTAN
Primary school enrollment: 93%
Population under 18: 30%
Total population: 15,422,000
Drawing: Firsova Katay, grade 4
Poetry: Habirova Maryam, grade 6
School: School nb. 79, Almaty
Translator: UNICEF Kazakhstan
Original text: Russian

KENYA
Primary school enrollment: 76%
Population under 18: 50%
Total population: 34,256,000
Drawing: Yvonne Khusoa, grade 4
Poetry: Aileen Nechesa, grade 4
School: Tumaini Miles of Smiles
School
Original text: English

KIRIBATI
Primary school enrollment: 97%
Population under 18: 39%
Total population: 99,000
Drawing: Caisilo, grade 7
Poetry: Bwetera, grade 7
School: War Memorial Primary
School
Translator: Laura Werner
Original text: Kiribati

KOREA, NORTH (DPRK)
Primary school enrollment: data not
available
Population under 18: 28%
Total population: 23,790,000
Drawing: Mun Hyok Jin, grade 6
Poetry: Kim Song, grade 3
Schools: Saenal Secondary School &
Runya Primary School
Translator: Koryo Tours
Original text: Korean

KOREA, SOUTH
Primary school enrollment: 99%
Population under 18: 23%
Total population: 47,817,000
Drawing: Lee Seung Hyun, grade 7
Poetry: Kim Min Ji, grade 7
School: SOS Children's Village
Translator: WooKang Yoon
Original text: Korean

KUWAIT
Primary school enrollment: 86%
Population under 18: 28%
Total population: 2,851,000
Drawing: Lolwa Adel, grade 2
Poetry: Dalal Al-Najm, grade 3
School: Sharmiya School Kuwait
Translator: Abderrahman El Mimouni
Original text: Arabic

KYRGYZSTAN
Primary school enrollment: 90%
Population under 18: 37%
Total population: 5,317,000
Drawing: Momun Kyzy Orozgul,
grade 8
Poetry: Aichurok Aijigitova, grade 8
School: Toguz-Bulak Secondary
School
Translator: Aslan Sydykov
Original text: Russian

LAOS
Primary school enrollment: 62%
Population under 18: 48%
Total population: 5,924,000
Drawing: Monethong, grade 6
Poetry: Vell Mane Phichid, grade 6
School: Children Education Centre
(C.E.C.), Vientiane
Translator: Sengdao Phonemany
Original text: Laotian

LATVIA
Primary school enrollment: data not
available
Population under 18: 19%
Total population: 2,307,000
Drawing: Vineta Silina, grade 3
Poetry: Martens Ribaks, grade 4
School: Bernu Nams "Imanta"
Orphanage
Translator: Signija Aizpuriete
Original text: Latvian

LEBANON
Primary school enrollment: 93%
Population under 18: 34%
Total population: 3,577,000
Drawing: Line Itani & Myriam Ali
Ahmad, grade 4
Poetry: Malek Kaedkey, grade 4
School: College Protestant Français
Translator: Katia Van de Putte
Original text: French

LESOTHO
Primary school enrollment: 65%
Population under 18: 47%
Total population: 2,008,000
Drawing: Teboho Lekhoti, grade 6
Poetry: Liengoane Malefane, grade 4
School: Hoohlo Primary School
Translator: The school
Original text: Sesotho

LIBERIA
Primary school enrollment: 66%
Population under 18: 54%
Total population: 3,283,000
Drawing: Edward Blackie
Poetry: Amunee Wheremonger
School: Child Art Liberia
Original text: English

LIBYA
Primary school enrollment: data not
available
Population under 18: 36%
Total population: 5,853,000
Drawing: Leila Buzrigh, grade 4
Poetry: Mahmoud Majblar, grade 4
School: Ecole Primaire de la
Communaute Francaise (MLF)
Translator: Stéphanie Rabemiafara
Original text: French

LIECHTENSTEIN
Primary school enrollment: 88%
Population under 18: 20%
Total population: 35,000
Drawing: Nadine Kolbener, grade 6
Poetry: Laura de Icco, grade 6
School: Triesen Primary School
Translator: Marcia Martinez
Original text: German

LITHUANIA
Primary school enrollment: 89%
Population under 18: 22%
Total population: 3,431,000
Drawing: Antano Vienudio, grade 5
Poetry: Viktorija Jilobrit, grade 5
School: Vilnius Antanas Vienuolis
Secondary School
Translator: Evelina Sernaite
Original text: Lithuanian

LUXEMBOURG
Primary school enrollment: 91%
Population under 18: 22%
Total population: 467,000
Drawing: Joshua Defays & Sarah
Schmitz, grade 4
Poetry: Joshua Defays, grade 4
Schools: Centre Scolaire Op Acker &
Centre Scolaire Am Sand
Translator: Renée Lippert-Weiler
Original text: Luxembourgish

MACEDONIA (FYROM)
Primary school enrollment: 92%
Population under 18: 24%
Total population: 2,034,000
Drawing: Alexander Bogoevski, grade 5
Poetry: Zoran Boshkov, grade 4
Schools: SOS Children's Village & Goce Delcev Elementary School
Translator: Irena Dodevska
Original text: Macedonian

MADAGASCAR
Primary school enrollment: 76%
Population under 18: 51%
Total population: 18,606,000
Drawing: Soa Aime Tafita Razafindravola, grade 5
Poetry: Michael Parfait Andrianjaka, grade 6
School: Ecole Primaire Publique d'Amondra
Translator: Cyrus Parfait
Original text: Malagasy

MALAWI
Primary school enrollment: 82%
Population under 18: 54%
Total population: 12,884,000
Drawing: Dalitso Phri, grade 8
Poetry: Rosemin Daud, grade 8
School: Kafulu Primary School
Original text: English

MALAYSIA
Primary school enrollment: 93%
Population under 18: 38%
Total population: 25,347,000
Drawing: Lim Sook Teng, grade 4
Poetry: Shi Ying, grade 3
School: Stella Maris Primary School
Original text: English

MALDIVES
Primary school enrollment: 90%
Population under 18: 40%
Total population: 306,000
Drawing: Mariyam Naba Nizam, grade 5
Poetry: Alya Ali Rasheed, grade 4
School: NCA Art Class
Original text: English

MALI
Primary school enrollment: 39%
Population under 18: 55%
Total population: 13,518,000
Drawing: Various students, grade 3
Poetry: Moulaye Farota, grade 4
School: Banankoro Fundamental School & Ngoa Primary School
Translator: Stéphanie Bourassa
Original text: Bambara

MALTA
Primary school enrollment: 94%
Population under 18: 21%
Total population: 407,000
Drawing: Sonja Altzinger, grade 4
Poetry: Luke Aaroh & Lucas Borg, grade 4
School: San Andrea School
Translator: The school
Original text: Maltese

MARSHALL ISLANDS
Primary school enrollment: 90%
Population under 18: 39%
Total population: 62,000
Drawing: Randon Jack, grade 4
Poetry: Julie An Ritok, grade 6
School: Majuro Cooperative School
Original text: English

MAURITANIA
Primary school enrollment: 44%
Population under 18: 46%
Total population: 3,124,000
Drawing: Various students, grade 5
Poetry: Mustafa Bochra, grade 6
School: Abi Houraira
Translator: Hana Bel Hadj Rhouma
Original text: Arabic

MAURITIUS
Primary school enrollment: 95%
Population under 18: 28%
Total population: 1,262,000
Drawing: Dierto Boulaye, grade 6
Poetry: Laurent Laventure, grade 6
School: Ecole de notre dame de Fatima
Translator: Stéphanie Rabemiafara
Original text: French

MEXICO
Primary school enrollment: 98%
Population under 18: 35%
Total population: 106,535,000
Drawing: Ricardo Daniel Pinto Mendoza, grade 8
Poetry: Maria Magdalena Vargas, grade 8
Schools: Petersen School & Colegio Los Charcos
Translator: Stéphanie Rabemiafara
Original text: Spanish

MICRONESIA
Primary school enrollment: data not available
Population under 18: 46%
Total population: 110,000
Drawing: Naidan Brady Perman, grade 9
Poetry: Karla Capelle, grade 4
Schools: PICS High School & Calvary Christian Academy Primary School
Original text: English

MOLDOVA
Primary school enrollment: 86%
Population under 18: 24%
Total population: 4,206,000
Drawing: Balan Anastasia, grade 4
Poetry: Cristina Socoliuc, grade 4
School: Pas o Pas (Step by Step ISSA) School
Translator: Maria Garstea
Original text: Moldovan

MONACO
Primary school enrollment: data not available
Population under 18: 18%
Total population: 33,000
Drawing: Arnaud, grade 3
Poetry: Stéphane, grade 3
School: FANB Monaco
Translator: Stéphanie Rabemiafara
Original text: French

MONGOLIA
Primary school enrollment: 84%
Population under 18: 34%
Total population: 2,629,000
Drawing: Enkhbayar Khaliun, grade 3
Poetry: S. Bayasgalan, grade 3
School: Bolovsrol complex
Translator: UNICEF Mongolia
Original text: Mongolian

MONTENEGRO
Primary school enrollment: data not available
Population under 18: 24%
Total population: 598,000
Drawing: Stela Bobot, grade 4
Poetry: Nikola Markus, grade 4
School: Primary School Stampr Makhrike
Translator: Atila Seke
Original text: Serbian

MOROCCO
Primary school enrollment: 86%
Population under 18: 35%
Total population: 31,224,000
Drawing: Mimouh Taher, grade 6
Poetry: Hoda el Kasbaoui, grade 6
School: Boulad Sguir Primary School
Translator: Soufiane Kennous
Original text: Arabic

MOZAMBIQUE
Primary school enrollment: 60%
Population under 18: 51%
Total population: 19,792,000
Drawing: Amad Silverio & Mateus Carlos, grade 3 & 5
Poetry: Quinteira Amelia Jamine, grade 5
School: Escola Primaria 25 de Junio
Translator: Rafael Pires
Original text: Portuguese

MYANMAR
Primary school enrollment: 84%
Population under 18: 36%
Total population: 50,519,000
Drawing: Various children, grade 4
Poetry: Various children, grade 5
School: Myanmar Buddhist Orphanage Association
Translator: Ko Ko Gyi
Original text: Burmese

NAMIBIA
Primary school enrollment: 74%
Population under 18: 45%
Total population: 2,074,000
Drawing: Hatani Tsuses, grade 5
Poetry: Ester Akweenda, grade 5
Schools: People Primary School &
Liina Mugano Orphanage
Original text: English

NAURU
Primary school enrollment: data not
available
Population under 18: 36%
Total population: 14,000
Drawing: Heartson Scotty, grade 5
Poetry: Ancine Dageago, grade 5
School: Nauru College
Original text: English

NEPAL
Primary school enrollment: 78%
Population under 18: 46%
Total population: 27,133,000
Drawing: Krishna Tamang, grade 6
Poetry: Saroj Rai, grade 5
School: CWIN Center for Children
at Risk
Translator: Rupa Joshi
Original text: Nepali

NETHERLANDS
Primary school enrollment: 99%
Population under 18: 22%
Total population: 16,419,000
Drawing: Jenny, grade 6
Poetry: Jaïro, grade 6
School: de Straap Openbare
Basisschool
Translator: Katia Vandeputte
Original text: Dutch

NEW ZEALAND
Primary school enrollment: 99%
Population under 18: 26%
Total population: 4,028,000
Drawing: Zoe Vaunois, grade 3
Poetry: Helena Douglas Thomson,
grade 4
School: St. Joseph Primary School
Original text: English

NICARAGUA
Primary school enrollment: 80%
Population under 18: 44%
Total population: 5,603,000
Drawing: Geovanny Mairena Paz,
grade 5
Poetry: Maria Diaz Rodriguez,
grade 6
School: Colegio El Portillo
Translator: Jakob Hans Renpening
Original text: Spanish

NIGER
Primary school enrollment: 30%
Population under 18: 56%
Total population: 13,957,000
Drawing: Madjid Aboubacar
Mamane, grade 4
Poetry: Rabi Sami, grade 6
Schools: French Primary School La
Poudriere III Primary School
Translator: Melissa Rice
Original text: French

NIGERIA
Primary school enrollment: 60%
Population under 18: 51%
Total population: 131,530,000
Drawing: Patricia Yusuf, Amina
Maruna, Victor Akan, Temple Adejo,
Cherub Henry, Chioma Aruabuike, &
Nathaniel Chukwuma, grade 6
Poetry: Fatih Okwudire, Fatimah
Abubakar, Philip Dada, Augustina
Haruna, Hapsat Adam, John Siaka, &
Efosa Imade, grade 6
School: Rantya School
Original text: English

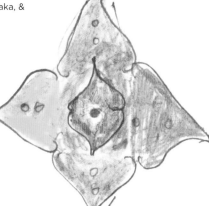

NORWAY
Primary school enrollment: 99%
Population under 18: 23%
Total population: 4,698,000
Drawing: Ingrid Klemmetvold,
grade 3
Poetry: Maren Kikhus, grade 3
School: Røros Primary School
Translator: Berit Indset
Original text: Norwegian

OMAN
Primary school enrollment: 78%
Population under 18: 39%
Total population: 2,595,000
Drawing: Various students, grade 4
Poetry: Ilyas, grade 4
School: Al Basayr School
Translator: Ghalia Hachem
Original text: Arabic

PAKISTAN
Primary school enrollment: 56%
Population under 18: 45%
Total population: 157,935,000
Drawing: Madiha, grade 6
Poetry: Madeeha Aslam, grade 5
School: Govt. Girls Elementary
School
Translator: School teachers
Original text: Urdu

PALAU
Primary school enrollment: 96%
Population under 18: 40%
Total population: 20,000
Drawing: Morisang, Charity, Lalii,
Duraimu, Turang, Mario, Marvin,
Darek, Texxon, & Arant, grade 6
Poetry: Students of grade 5
School: Koror Primary School
Original text: English

PANAMA
Primary school enrollment: 98%
Population under 18: 36%
Total population: 3,232,000
Drawing: Alabrades de Leon, grade 3
Poetry: Katherine Gustavino, grade 5
School: Escuela Emperatriz Taboada
Translator: Stéphanie Rabemiafara
Original text: Spanish

PAPUA NEW GUINEA
Primary school enrollment: data not
available
Population under 18: 47%
Total population: 5,887,000
Drawing: Kokenu Makita, grade 6
Poetry: Rolly Elivap, grade 6
School: Wardstrip Primary School
Original text: English

PARAGUAY
Primary school enrollment: 96%
Population under 18: 44%
Total population: 6,158,000
Drawing: Tania Franco, grade 5
Poetry: Maria Magdalena Ocampos,
grade 6
School: Escuela Ignacio A. Pane,
grade 6
Translator: Stéphanie Rabemiafara
Original text: Spanish

PERU
Primary school enrollment: 97%
Population under 18: 38%
Total population: 27,968,000
Drawing: Janin Saranga, grade 3
Poetry: Aracelli Reyme Alegria,
grade 8
School: Escuela Secondaria
Translator: Agustina Dillon
Original text: Spanish

PHILIPPINES
Primary school enrollment: 88%
Population under 18: 42%
Total population: 83,054,000
Drawing: Lally R. Rosales, grade 5
Poetry: Akito Marc T. Irave Jr,
grade 6
School: Culiat Elementary School
Translator: John Williams
Original text: Tagalog

POLAND
Primary school enrollment: 97%
Population under 18: 21%
Total population: 38,530,000
Drawing: Joanna Dabrowska,
grade 6
Poetry: Wronika Karska, grade 3
School: Szkoly Podstawowej nb. 62
Translator: Kamila Kielar
Original text: Polish

PORTUGAL
Primary school enrollment: 99%
Population under 18: 19%
Total population: 10,495,000
Drawing: Madalena, grade 3
Poetry: Neuza Sanches, grade 4
School: Centro Social e Paroquial
de Sao Maximiliano Kolbe, Centro
Social Bairro 6 de Maio
Translator: Anthony Asael
Original text: Portuguese

QATAR
Primary school enrollment: 95%
Population under 18: 25%
Total population: 841,000
Drawing: Hessa Nasser, grade 3
Poetry: Fatima Hani Hussain, grade 5
School: Newton International School
Original text: English

ROMANIA
Primary school enrollment: 92%
Population under 18: 20%
Total population: 21,711,000
Drawing: Barbu Bianca, grade 6
Poetry: Barbu Diana, grade 6
School: Colegio National Fratii
Buzesti
Translator: Andreea Ciobanu
Original text: Romanian

RUSSIA
Primary school enrollment: 91%
Population under 18: 19%
Total population: 142,499,000
Drawing: Barbara Lemrachyk, grade 5
Poetry: Daniel Tenyakov, grade 6
Schools: Petrischule 222 & Gymnasium 209
Translator: Maria Steffee
Original text: Russian

RWANDA
Primary school enrollment: 73%
Population under 18: 52%
Total population: 9,038,000
Drawing: Nicole Muhawenimana, grade 3
Poetry: Lionel Mbarubucyeye, grade 3
School: Ecole La Colombiere
Translator: Stéphanie Rabemiafara
Original text: French

SAINT KITTS & NEVIS
Primary school enrollment: 94%
Population under 18: 34%
Total population: 50,000
Drawing: Diahon Jung, grade 4
Poetry: Jevaughn Brown, grade 5
School: Estridge Primary School
Original text: English

SAINT LUCIA
Primary school enrollment: 98%
Population under 18: 33%
Total population: 165,000
Drawing: Dylan Singh, grade 5
Poetry: Sabina Labadie, grade 5
School: Ti Rocher Primary School
Original text: English

SAINT VINCENT & THE GRENADINES
Primary school enrollment: 94%
Population under 18: 35%
Total population: 120,000
Drawing: Ashini Best, grade 5
Poetry: Vaughan Russell, grade 5
Schools: Sugarmill Academy & Calliqua Primary School
Original text: English

SAMOA
Primary school enrollment: 90%
Population under 18: 48%
Total population: 185,000
Drawing: Jacob Anvaa, grade 4
Poetry: Tuposiliva, grade 6
School: Vaimoso Primary School
Original text: English

SAN MARINO
Primary school enrollment: data not available
Population under 18: 18%
Total population: 28,000
Drawing: Andreani Sara, Di Silvestri Elisa, grade 4
Poetry: Cecilia Busignani, grade 4
School: Scuolas Elementares di San Marino
Translator: UNICEF San Marino
Original text: Italian

SAO TOME & PRINCIPE
Primary school enrollment: 84%
Population under 18: 46%
Total population: 157,000
Drawing: Alimary Patricia, grade 3
Poetry: Bruno Cardoso, grade 4
School: Escola Dona Maria de Jesus
Translator: Jessica Meoni
Original text: Portuguese

SAUDI ARABIA
Primary school enrollment: 59%
Population under 18: 40%
Total population: 24,735,000
Drawing: Faisal al Yahya, grade 5
Poetry: Mohd Bander al Saud, grade 5
School: King Faisal School
Translator: Hana Bel Hadj Rhouma
Original text: Arabic

SENEGAL
Primary school enrollment: 66%
Population under 18: 50%
Total population: 11,658,000
Drawing: Cheikh Fadel Sakho, grade 4
Poetry: Khalifa Cisse, grade 4
School: École Liberté 6 A
Translator: Stéphanie Bourassa
Original text: French

SERBIA
Primary school enrollment: 95%
Population under 18: 22%
Total population: 9,858,000
Drawing: Miagen Pojobuth, grade 4
Poetry: Inic Dragana, grade 4
School: "Miloš Crnjanski" Primary School & "Miloš Antic" Primary School
Translator: Senka Obrodovic-Smuk
Original text: Serbian

SEYCHELLES
Primary school enrollment: 96%
Population under 18: 51%
Total population: 87,000
Drawing: Julio Morel, grade 5
Poetry: Valentina Vidot, grade 5
School: Baie Lazare School
Translator: Bernadette Dogley
Original text: Creole

SIERRA LEONE
Primary school enrollment: 41%
Population under 18: 49%
Total population: 5,525,000
Drawing: Jauda A. Fullah, grade 5
Poetry: Abu B. Marrah, grade 5
School: Sierra Leone Muslim Brotherhood School
Original text: English

SINGAPORE
Primary school enrollment: data not available
Population under 18: 24%
Total population: 4,326,000
Drawing: Lin Xin Yan, grade 4
Poetry: Various students, grade 4
Schools: Saint Stephen School & Stamford Primary School
Original text: English

SLOVAKIA
Primary school enrollment: data not available
Population under 18: 21%
Total population: 5,401,000
Drawing: Lukas Ljubovic, grade 3
Poetry: Barbora Simkovicová, grade 3
School: ZS Pankúchova 4 BA
Translator: Zuzana Cacova
Original text: Slovak

SLOVENIA
Primary school enrollment: 98%
Population under 18: 18%
Total population: 1,967,000
Drawing: Enya Belak, grade 7
Poetry: Neza Bregar, grade 7
School: Primary school BICEVJE
Translator: Alenka Gnezda
Original text: Slovene

SOLOMON ISLANDS
Primary school enrollment: 80%
Population under 18: 47%
Total population: 478,000
Drawing: Remmey, grade 3
Poetry: Various students, grade 3
School: St. Nicolas School
Original text: English

SOMALIA
Primary school enrollment: 12%
Population under 18: 50%
Total population: 8,699,000
Drawing: Khadra Axmed, grade 7
Poetry: Saamiya Axmed, grade 7
School: Dugsiga Nasaablood
Translator: Mr. Abdi
Original text: Somali

SOUTH AFRICA
Primary school enrollment: 89%
Population under 18: 38%
Total population: 48,577,000
Drawing: Lizen Pan, grade 3
Poetry: Hemal Prag, grade 3
Schools: Lebo's backpacker children center & St. John's Preparatory School
Original text: English

SPAIN
Primary school enrollment: 99%
Population under 18: 17%
Total population: 43,064,000
Drawing: Marta Morena, grade 3
Poetry: Silvia, grade 4
School: Doctor Azua School
Translator: Ania Delia Gonzalez
Original text: Spanish

SRI LANKA
Primary school enrollment: 99%
Population under 18: 29%
Total population: 19,299,000
Drawing: Dinithi Navodya Lanarol, grade 5
Poetry: Vinuja Vihansith Jayasinhe, grade 3
School: Lanka Saba Junior School
Translator: A.G.N. Sudath
Original text: Sinhala

SUDAN
Primary school enrollment: 58%
Population under 18: 47%
Total population: 38,560,000
Drawing: Saba Mubarak, grade 4
Poetry: Hager Adam, grade 4
School: Al Malaz School
Translator: Abdelwahab Ali Mohamedc
Original text: Arabic

SURINAME
Primary school enrollment: 92%
Population under 18: 36%
Total population: 449,000
Drawing: Gwendelien Alboltol, grade 5
Poetry: Roslie Kentie, grade 5
School: Brokopondo Primary School
Translator: School teachers
Original text: Sranan Tongo

SWAZILAND
Primary school enrollment: 77%
Population under 18: 50%
Total population: 1,032,000
Drawing: Nkosikhona Dlamini, grade 5
Poetry: Lungile Shongwe, grade 6
School: SOS Children's Village Mbabane
Original text: English

SWEDEN
Primary school enrollment: 99%
Population under 18: 21%
Total population: 9,041,000
Drawing: Amanda, grade 5
Poetry: Sara, grade 5
School: Annelundsskolan
Translator: Andreas Johansson
Original text: Swedish

SWITZERLAND
Primary school enrollment: 94%
Population under 18: 20%
Total population: 7,252,000
Drawing:Melanie Oppliger, grade 7
Poetry: Sarina, Maja, Carmen, & Nina, grade 6
School: Primarschule Herrenhof & Uzeschuel Kirchstrasse
Translator: Marcia Martinez
Original text: German

SYRIA
Primary school enrollment: 95%
Population under 18: 44%
Total population: 19,043,000
Drawing: Sarah Safi, grade 4
Poetry: Mohammed Joudeh, grade 5
School: Tatbikat Maslakya School
Translator: School teachers
Original text: Arabic

TAJIKISTAN
Primary school enrollment: 89%
Population under 18: 46%
Total population: 6,736,000
Drawing: Marufjon Faiziboev, grade 5
Poetry: Nigora Mahmudova, grade 6
Schools: Gymmasium nb. 2 Khojand & Shing Village School
Translator: Umed Kurbanov
Original text: Russian

TANZANIA
Primary school enrollment: 73%
Population under 18: 51%
Total population: 40,454,000
Drawing: Dauda Rajabu, grade 5
Poetry: Aristides Audax, grade 5
School: Nyakabungo Primary School
Translator: Hassan Wanini
Original text: Swahili

THAILAND
Primary school enrollment: data not available
Population under 18: 29%
Total population: 64,233,000
Drawing: Kanthisak Signpho, Kornthep Kryaksorn, Jettarin Ponrasak, Thanakorn Jirawatthanawichan, & Suthasit Jirawatthanawichan, grade 6
Poetry: Nirutchaya Chumkrin, Piyaporn Inpram, & Yongmee Wutcharapon, grade 6
School: Chumphon Municipality School (Ban-ta-ta-pao)
Translator: Paul Klongboon
Original text: Thai

TIMOR-LESTE
Primary school enrollment: 75%
Population under 18: 49%
Total population: 947,000
Drawing: Celestina Ximenes, grade 5
Poetry: Jose Carlos, grade 6
School: Escola Primaria Santa Madalena de Canossa
Translator: Jose Ximenes
Original text: Tetum

TOGO
Primary school enrollment: 70%
Population under 18: 50%
Total population: 6,145,000
Drawing: Seshie Mawuko, grade 5
Poetry: Akossiwa Stella, grade 4
Schools: Private School Academie H. Aboni. Le Corridor du Succes School
Translator: Melissa Rice
Original text: French

TONGA
Primary school enrollment: 91%
Population under 18: 42%
Total population: 102,000
Drawing: Margaret Uata, grade 6
Poetry: Taina Puloka, grade 6
School: Tonga Side School
Original text: English

TRINIDAD & TOBAGO
Primary school enrollment: 92%
Population under 18: 27%
Total population: 1,333,000
Drawing: Kristen Hannywell, grade 3
Poetry: Gabriel Vieira, grade 3
School: Bishop Anstey Junior School
Original text: English

TUNISIA
Primary school enrollment: 97%
Population under 18: 31%
Total population: 10,327,000
Drawing: Haythem Taboubi, grade 6
Poetry: Nesrine Amiri, grade 6
School: Bardo Scout Group
Translator: Hafedh Messaoudi
Original text: Arabic

TURKEY
Primary school enrollment: 89%
Population under 18: 33%
Total population: 74,877,000
Drawing: Sena Olgun, grade 5
Poetry: Merve Özdil, grade 5
School: Bilfen Kosuyolu School
Translator: Aylin Yengin
Original text: Turkish

TURKMENISTAN
Primary school enrollment: 76%
Population under 18: 37%
Total population: 4,965,000
Drawing: Fusyipewa Lagyn, grade 7
Poetry: Maksat Pendiyew, grade 5
School: Ruhnama School
Translator: Ayna Seyitlieva
Original text: Turkmen

TUVALU
Primary school enrollment: data not available
Population under 18: 40%
Total population: 10,000
Drawing: Emily Kapuafe, grade 4
Poetry: Tau Penehuro, grade 4
School: Government Primary School
Original text: English

UGANDA
Primary school enrollment: 87%
Population under 18: 57%
Total population: 28,816,000
Drawing: Kiyingi Akisam, grade 6
Poetry: Musa Sultan, grade 6
School: Nakivubo Primary School
Original text: English

UKRAINE
Primary school enrollment: 82%
Population under 18: 18%
Total population: 46,205,000
Drawing: Sasha Alekseeva, grade 6
Poetry: Taras Kravchenko, grade 6
School: Specialized ASPnet UNESCO School 211
Translator: Irina Kuznetsova
Original text: Ukrainian

UNITED ARAB EMIRATES
Primary school enrollment: 71%
Population under 18: 23%
Total population: 4,380,000
Drawing: Tommy Bodo, grade 3
Poetry: Sophie, grade 3
School: Universal American School
Original text: English

UNITED KINGDOM
Primary school enrollment: 99%
Population under 18: 22%
Total population: 59,668,000
Drawing: Jeremy Rees, grade 4
Poetry: Fraser, grade 4
School: Eltham Primary School
Original text: English

UNITED STATES OF AMERICA
Primary school enrollment: 92%
Population under 18: 25%
Total population: 298,213,000
Drawing: Sharon K., grade 5
Poetry: A.J. Smith, grade 5
School: Ribet Academy
Original text: English

URUGUAY
Primary school enrollment: 100%
Population under 18: 29%
Total population: 3,463,000
Drawing: Vanessa Franco Diaz, grade 4
Poetry: Leonardo Mara, grade 4
School: Escuela 163
Translator: Stéphanie Rabemiafara
Original text: Spanish

UZBEKISTAN
Primary school enrollment: 95%
Population under 18: 39%
Total population: 27,372,000
Drawing: Rahmanova Zebo, grade 4
Poetry: Abdullaev Artur, grade 4
School: School nb. 40 Parvoz
Translator: The school
Original text: Russian

VANUATU
Primary school enrollment: 94%
Population under 18: 47%
Total population: 211,000
Drawing: Marie Namak, grade 7
Poetry: Marie Williams, grade 7
School: Melapoa College
Original text: English

VENEZUELA
Primary school enrollment: 92%
Population under 18: 37%
Total population: 26,749,000
Drawing: Mary Evelyn Barroso, grade 6
Poetry: Andrea Ortega, grade 6
School: Centro de Educación Popular de Santa Rosa de Agua, Maracaibo
Translator: Katia Vandeputte
Original text: Spanish

VIETNAM
Primary school enrollment: 94%
Population under 18: 36%
Total population: 84,238,000
Drawing: Nguyen Ai Q Nhu, grade 6
Poetry: Kim Phuong, grade 3
Schools: Phan Tay Ho Primary School & Hermann Gmeiner School
Translator: School teachers
Original text: Vietnamese

YEMEN
Primary school enrollment: 75%
Population under 18: 52%
Total population: 22,389,000
Drawing: Fatima Ahmed, grade 7
Poetry: Eman Abado, grade 6
School: Sanham School
Translator: Najla Alshami
Original text: Arabic

ZAMBIA
Primary school enrollment: 57%
Population under 18: 53%
Total population: 11,668,000
Drawing: Various students, grade 3
Poetry: Steven Muiega, grade 6
School: Aisha Project School
Original text: English

ZIMBABWE
Primary school enrollment: 82%
Population under 18: 48%
Total population: 13,010,000
Drawing: Synodia, grade 5
Poetry: Brighton Chovunita, grade 5
School: Mavombo Learning Center
Original text: English

Acknowledgments

We want to express our immense gratitude to the people, institutions, and businesses that contributed funds, work, ideas, encouragement, and affection for the success of this project.

A special thank you to all the children whom we have met in our workshops— for their joy, enthusiasm, creativity, and generosity.

Thank you to the teachers and schools that believed in us and opened their doors, for their trust and collaboration.

Thank you to SOS Children's Villages for receiving us so warmly in eleven of their villages.

Thank you to the hundreds of local NGOs (Non-Governmental Organizations) that gave us help and support.

Thank you to UNICEF and Fundación América for your valuable cooperation and support, and for granting us your trust since our very first steps.

Thank you to the hundreds of volunteers who held out their hands throughout the world: on-site producers, translators, sponsors, and supportive people who gave us financial contributions and welcomed us in their houses.

And thank you to our families for having raised us with freedom and the capacity to dream and believe that we can reach our dreams.

Our Volunteers

Algeria: Nadjib Benyoucef; **Andorra:** Tania Verges; **Angola:** Constantino Luciano; **Argentina:** Luis Gabardini, Vicky Galmarini; **Armenia:** Zara Ohanyan; **Australia:** Louis Philippe Loncke, Rebecca Wyles, Rhonda & Vito Brown; **Austria:** Philippe & Maud Poschelle, Martin Gloeckler; **Azerbaijan:** Anar Gurbanov; **Bahamas:** Cathy Legrand, Melissa Groff; **Bahrain:** Ipshita Sen; **Belarus:** Milla Yarmakovich; **Belgium:** Alain Castermans, Ann Verbeke, Audrey Kindt, Daphnee Parre, Delphine Moerenhout, Dominique Bonte, Enrica Nardello, Eva Valle, Florence Bondue, Gaelle Jacques, Graziella Lippolis , Hector Martin, Jerome Waterkeyn, Kerenn Elkaim, Laurent Poznantek, Maja Slegers, Max Bentickx, Michael Jacobs, Pascal Musch, Patricia Willocq, Ronny Wagemans, Sabrina Foroncelli, Veronique Urbain, Yvette Haker, Louis Philippe Loncke, Nicolas Janssen, Sandra Farana, Audrey Hausman, Emilie Bertrand, Noelle Ghislain, Jean Yves de Jaucot, Delphine Menard, Veronique Pochet, Bjorn Accoe; **Belize:** Daniel Velasquez; **Benin:** Francois Godonou; **Bolivia:** Edgar Aruquipa Chambi, Marcia Martinez; **Botswana:** Tommy Hamaluba; Brazil: Adriana Cassaroti, Andrea Casarotti, Silvia dos Santos, Patricia Nascimento Delorme, Lirian Monteiro; **Brunei:** Paul Liew; **Bulgaria:** Petrov Vesselin; **Burkina Faso:** Abdulaye Sawadogo, Romuald Compaore, Sylvie André-Dumont; **Burundi:** Aimé Muganga, Yvonne Marorerwa; **Canada:** Mandy Goodgoll, Marta Borowski, Rochelle Michaels, Tabish Bhimani; **Central African Republic:** Patrick Asael; **Chile:** Andres Cargill, Francisco Pezo, Michael Stone; **China:** Fabrice & Mylene Marcotty, Sarah Feng; **Colombia:** Alfredo Hernandez, Gloria Vallejo, Kelly Villalobos; **Costa Rica:** Alejandra Carvajal Vallejos, Marcia Martinez; **Cote d'Ivoire:** Mandjouh Touré; **Croatia:** Ivana Boras; **Cuba:** Graziella Lippolis; **Czech Republic:** Llenka Naceradska; **Democratic Republic of Congo:** Bangala Family; **Denmark:** Lassina Badolo, Lisa Hartmann Andersen, Mette Walsted, Maria Hansen, Mikkel Preisler; **Dominica:** Anna McCanse; **Dominican Republic:** Luis Quiñones, Pedro F. Joseph; **El Salvador:** Marcia Martinez; **Ethiopia:** Michael Araya, Sonya & Bob Hedley; **Finland:** Jonna Kilkki; **France:** Aline Rodriguez, Ludovic Hubler, Magali Fourmaintraux, Sophie Fromental & Denis Cantin, Sophie & Carsten Walenda, Macarena Dupouy, Marion Prats; **Gabon:** Paul Avougou; **Germany:** Thorsten & Anne Ulbrich; **Greece:** Sofia Kouvelaki; **Guatemala:** Marcia Martínez; **Guinea:** Frere Stephane Léon; **Honduras:** Marcia Martinez; **India:** Biplop Dutta, Anamika Mehta; **Indonesia:** Shanna Wulandaru; **Iraq:** Anthony Legg; **Ireland:** Dara Connoly; **Israel:** Roee Pekin; **Italy:** Barbara Morana, Loredana Sementini, Lisa Tucci, Tania Klein, Valentina Cassata; **Japan:** Benoit Olivier, Kazue Ihobe; **Kenya:** Rose Bugusu; **Laos:** Jo Pereira; **Latvia:** Ieva Jurkele, Signija Aizpuriete; **Libya:** Reghad Hussein; **Lichtenstein:** Kerstin Kaiser; **Luxembourg:** Rosemarie Rohmer; **Madagascar:** Martine Catry; **Malaysia:** Valentina Cassata; **Maldives:** Shani Ahmed, Noorulla Mohamed, Ahmad Nimad; **Malta:** James Martin; **Mauritius:** Nicholas Rainer; **Mexico:** Alejandro Quiroz, Marcia Martinez, Rodrigo Jardón; **Micronesia:** Joseph Diaz; **Monaco:** Medecin Family; **Morocco:** Delphine Delire, Fatiha Messoud; **Namibia:** Matthias Langheld; **Netherlands:** Andy Zijlmans, Maresa Sprietsma, Nathalie Bovenberg; **New Zealand:** Arnnei Speiser, Linda Farr, Vivienne Wright; **Niger:** Bachir Aboubacar; **Nigeria:** Thomas Dedouhet, Emilia Eyo; **North Korea:** Hannah Barraclough, Gopalan Balagopal; **Norway:** Berit Indset; **Pakistan:** Tabish Bhimani; **Palau:** Caleb Otto; **Panama:** Marcia Martinez; **Papua New Guinea:** Joshua Jackson; **Paraguay:** Gabriel Van Dyck, Ricardo Ruiz Diaz; **Philippines:** Factora Family; **Poland:** Kamila Kielar, Magda Nowacka; **Qatar:** Susanna Wallis; **Romania:** Andreea Ciobanu; **Russia:** Lilya Chichevatkina, Marina Zyazina; **Serbia:** Aleksandra Kostic; **Seychelles:** Bernadette Dogley; **Singapore:** Sabrina Wan, Valentina Cassata, Harisson Goh; **South Africa:** Anne Catherine Schaub, Sally Dore, Virginie Caura; **Spain:** Elena Gimenez, Felix Slager & Valerie Lamy, Sonia Hernando, Alejandra Garcia; **St. Kitts & Nevis:** Amber Greening, Martha Landis; **St. Lucia:** Darius Lafeuillee, Lee Klejnot; **St. Vincent & The Grenadines:** Helena Nyhlen; **Sudan:** Violetta Polese; **Suriname:** Sue Reuther; **Sweden:** Åsa Qvarnström, Eva Missler, Dennis Rodie; **Switzerland:** Marcia Martinez, Thomas Jenni, Laïla von Alvensleben; **Tanzania:** Cyrille Falisse; **Thailand:** Francis Cripps, Paul Klongboon, K. Rajani; **Trinidad & Tobago:** Phyllis Hoyte; **Togo:** Max Claver; **Turkey:** Fatosh Munar, Levent Kormaz; **Uganda:** Mike Sembiro; **United Arab Emirates:** Regina Maniaci; **United Kingdom:** Grace Pattison, Miriam Leach, Ruth Wheeler, Vanessa Noublanche-Ottolenghi; **United States of America:** Ana Amélia Junqueira Prevatto, Caitlyn Carpanzano, Dana Curran, Danielle Kaniper, Jennifer Singer, Jessica Riley, Linda Tom, Mike Hulsey, Nellie Vishnevsky, Nishi Kothari, Phil Micali, Rochelle Michaels, Simon Suh, Marina Massi, Nishi Kothari, Shefali Murdia, Meredith Gonzalez, Sarah Helen Snow, Emily Witt; **Uruguay:** Irina Raffo; **Venezuela:** Fatima da Silva, Evelyn B. Cordova; **Yemen:** Charles Debras; **Zambia:** Matthew Brooke.

Our Translators

Afghanistan: Ahmad Seiar Razaie; **Algeria:** Nadjib Benyoucef; **Argentina:** Agustina Dillon, Lucia Manucci; **Armenia:** Mariam Sukhudyan; **Azerbaijan:** Anar Gurbanov; **Bangladesh:** Shantona Momtaz; **Belarus:** Natasha Vaitovich; **Belgium:** Birgit Van de Wijer, Ilona Mandl, Karla de Greef, Katia Vandeputte, Lya Judith Crivisqui, Michel Theissen, Muriel Rappaport, Nathalie Magosse, Pascale Croonenberghs, Patricia Quirk, Saskia Leeuwenhoek, Yvette Haker, Andre Ostachkov; **Bosnia & Herzegovina:** Ewa Golijanin; **Brazil:** Adriana Macias, Livia Ferolla, Lucia Nascimento, Elsa Viegas, Liliana Ribeiro, Olyntho Mentzingen, Suellen Aucejo; **Bulgaria:** Savina Bogoeva; **Chile:** Claudia Serey, Francisco Pezo, Jose Miguel Neira, Marcia Martinez; **China:** Sinba Duan; **Croatia:** Atila Seke, Kresimir Hrdlicka; **Cuba:** Ana Delia Gonzalez; **Cyprus:** Noni Xatzinikolaou; **Czech Republic:** Jana Reznícková; **Denmark:** Mette Walsted; **Egypt:** Hebattallah Ali; **El Salvador:** Rebeca Monge; **Eritrea:** Awet Araya Bahlbi; **Estonia:** Ms. Kerttu; **Finland:** Jonna Kilkki; **France:** Abderrahman El Mimouni, Cecilia Charpentier, Elodie Ollivier, Emilie Billon, Laure de Fabiani, Stephane Varman, Stephanie Bourassa, Erika & Baptiste Rosset; **Germany:** Kathryn Ryder, Maria Steffee; **Greece:** George S.; **Guatemala:** Janina Ralda de Castellanos; **Guinea:** Mariama Barry; **Hungary:** Katalin Dobrovotzky; **Iceland:** Birna Margrét Júlíusdóttir; **India:** Nibedita Sen, Sonal Jalan, Vinita Agarwal; **Indonesia:** Shanna Wulandru, Sigit Adinugroho; **Iraq:** Jehan Legg, Saleem Sadeeq Haji Al Zebari; **Israel:** Jonathan Howard, Roee Pekin; **Italy:** Elisa Capuano, Marco Marongiu; **Japan:** Yurika Mochizuki; **Jordan:** Rua Sharawi, Rula Abdel Hamid; **Kenya:** Hassan Wanini; **Kiribati:** Laura Werner; **Korea (South):** WooKang Yoon; **Kyrgyzstan:** Aslan Sydykov; **Laos:** Jo Pereira, Mingkhounakham Sisavath, Sengdao Phonemany; **Latvia:** Signiia Aizpuriete; **Lebanon:** Ghalia Hachem, Ludmila Bitar, Valia Baaklini; **Lithuania:** Evelina Sernaite, Tomasz Czepaitis; **Luxembourg:** Renée Lippert-Weiler; **Macedonia:** Bosko Stankovski, Irena Dodevska, Kristofer Jovkovski; **Madagascar:** Cécile Rasoamaharavo, Cyrus Parfait; **Malaysia:** Sianny Christanti; **Mexico:** Jakob Hans Renpening, Jorge Aleman; **Moldova:** Maria Garstea; **Morocco:** Soufiane Kennous; **Myanmar:** Ko Ko Gyi; **Nepal:** Rupa Joshi; **Netherlands:** Pryn Zijlmans; **Norway:** Berit Indset; **Philippines:** John Williams, Mylene Marcotty Pereira; **Poland:** Kamila Kielar, Paulina; **Portugal:** Joana Santos, Rafael Pires; **Romania:** Andreea Ciobanu; **Saudi Arabia:** Omar Behairy; **Serbia:** Dolores Gbric, Dule Jelen; **Seychelles:** Bernadette Dogley; **Slovakia:** Zuzana Cacová; **Slovenia:** Alenka Gnezda; **Somalia:** Mr. Abdi; **South Africa:** Richard Higgs; **Spain:** Eva Monzon, Susana Diaz; **Sri Lanka:** A.G.N. Sudath; **Sudan:** Abdelwahab Ali Mohamed; **Sweden:** Andreas Johansson, Åsa Qvarnström; **Tajikistan:** Umed Kurbanov; **Thailand:** Paul Klongboon; **Timor-Leste:** Jose Ximenes; **Tunisia:** Amira Belhani, Hafedh Messaoudi, Hana Bel Hadj Rhouma, Houeida Anouar; **Turkey:** Aylin Yengin, Esin Turkakin, Melih Ismail Inan, Melis Ari; **Turkmenistan:** Ayna Seyitlieva; **Ukraine:** Irina Kuznetsova, Tatiana Semenova; **United Arab Emirates:** Aisha Abbasi; **United Kingdom:** Jessica Hutchison, Tara Naval; **United States of America:** Belda Kosasih, Elizabeth Chatfield Vernier, Alisha Reaves, Alix Quan, Anna Bazhaw-Hyscher, Audrey Adams, Catherine Kennedy, Elizabeth McBean, Jenny Jonson, Jessica Meoni, Melia Albrecht, Melissa Rice, Patricia Brenes, Rebecca Gibergues, Tunisia Baker, Willow Paule; **Venezuela:** Blanca Strepponi, Fatima da Silva; **Yemen:** Najla Alshami.

Our Hosts

Albania: SOS Children's Village Tirana; **Algeria:** Benyoucef Family; **Andorra:** Tamara Paez; **Angola:** Peter Matz, Stephane Arnaud; **Argentina:** Luis Gabardini; **Armenia:** Mariam Sukhudyan; **Australia:** Cindy Veltens, George & Mairi, Louis Philippe Loncke, Rhonda & Vito Brown; **Austria:** Philippe & Maud Poschelle; **Azerbaijan:** Beatriz Romero; **Bahamas:** Cathy Legrand; **Bahrain:** Ipshita Sen; **Barbados:** Ana & Marc-Andre Lorrain; **Belarus:** Anton & Milla Yarmakovich; **Belgium:** Nirina Rabemiafara & Desire Magbunduku, Haker-Asael Family; **Belize:** Daniel Velasquez; **Benin:** Philippe & Lola Brossel; **Botswana:** Hamaluba Family; **Brazil:** Ana-Luiza & Rodrigo Fragoso, Michael Jackson Pimenta, Glaucia & Euripides Pinho, Junior Casarotti, Ribeiro-Casarotti Family; **Brunei:** Paul Liew; **Bulgaria:** Giorgev-Alexandrova Family; **Burundi:** Muganga Family; **Cambodia:** Noe-Wilson Family, SOS Children's Village Siem Reap; **Cameroon:** Joel Ibrahim Mahamat; **Canada:** Rochelle Michaels; **Central African Republic:** Patrick & Belinda Asael; **Chad:** Rados & Veronica Horacek-Gomez; **Chile:** Barbara Morana & Patrick Jadoul, Felipe Valenzuela, Luciana & Rodrigo Pino, Luis & Leslie Flores, Roberto Edwards; **China:** Fabrice & Mylene Marcotty, Francois Xavier Henry & Florence Paturel, Jean Van Wetter; **Colombia:** Raul Toro; **Congo:** Sylvie Niombo; **Costa Rica:** Alejandra Carvajal Vallejos; **Cote d'Ivoire:** Ali Konate; **Croatia:** Ivana Boras, John Obraz; **Cyprus:** Ingus & Lina Leitane; **Czech Republic:** Llenka Naceradska; **Democratic Republic of Congo:** Bangala Family; **Denmark:** Martin B. Braunstein, Mette Walsted; **Dominican Republic:** Angel Isaias Adames, Chantal & Ybo Bruijsten; **Dominica:** Anna McCanse; **Ecuador:** SOS Children's Village Ibarra; **Equatorial Guinea:** UNICEF; **Estonia:** Sergei Trofimov; **Ethiopia:** Hedley Family; **Fiji:** Tim Wilson; **Finland:** Anni Partanen, Jonna Kilkki; **France:** Eve & Romain Marigny, Bangala-Vergez Family, Soary Andrianarisoa, Sophie & Denis Cantin; **Gabon:** Edgar & Sylvie Nziembi Doukaga, UNICEF; **Georgia:** SOS Children's Village Tbilissi; **Germany:** Ulbrich Family; **Guatemala:** Percy Jacobs; **Guinea Bissau:** Farba Diouf; **Hungary:** Meier Family; **Iceland:** Ingimar Helgason, Setta & Bjarni Mortensen; **India:** Biplop Dutta, Durga Family, UNICEF Rajasthan; **Indonesia:** Wulandaru Family; **Iraq:** Jihan & Anthony Legg; **Iran:** Partovi Family; **Ireland:** Vesper, Robin & Brad, Lucia Greco; **Israel:** Eitan Haker; **Italy:** Lisa Tucci, Valentina Cassata; **Jamaica:** Amelia Scharrer; **Japan:** Benoit Olivier, Gabriel Santamarina, Ole Troan & Evangeline Manalac; **Kenya:** Rose Bugusu; **Kiribati:** Tierata & Laura Werner Family; **Korea (South):** Woo Kang Woon; **Kuwait:** Thomas Joseph; **Kyrgyzstan:** UNICEF; **Latvia:** Ieva Jurkele, Signija Aizpuriete; **Lebanon:** Roukoss Family; **Liechtenstein:** Kerstin Kaiser; **Lithuania:** Egle Satkute; **Luxembourg:** Sydson Marigny Family; **Macedonia:** Al Yates, SOS Children's Village Skopje; **Madagascar:** Martine Catry; **Malaysia:** Grace Looi; **Mali:** Academie d'Education Segou, Manssoul Bassoum; **Malta:** James Martin; **Marshall Islands:** Kathy & Jim Stratte; **Mauritius:** Nicholas Rainer; **Mexico:** Quiroz Family, Marylou & Jose Israel Capuano; **Moldova:** Irina Bulat; **Monaco:** Medecin Family; **Mongolia:** UNICEF; **Morocco:** Belamime Family; **Mozambique:** Bryant Hobgood Family; **Namibia:** Matthias Langheld; **Netherlands:** Zijlmans Family; **New Zealand:** Vivienne Wright; **Niger:** Bachir & Miriam Aboubacar Mamane; **Nigeria:** Jennifer Brinkerhoff, Thomas & Sam Dedouhet; **Norway:** Sigurd Nielsen; **Oman:** Daniel Jendrissek; **Papua New Guinea:** Joshua Jackson, Margaret Cubani; **Paraguay:** Ricardo Ruiz Diaz; **Peru:** Carlos Medina; **Philippines:** Factora Family, Henry-Paturel Family, Martine Catry; **Portugal:** Marta Lopes; **Qatar:** Trevor Ryan; **Romania:** Ciobanu Family; **Russia:** Lilya Chichevatkina; **Rwanda:** Irene Odera; **San Marino:** Claudia Guidi; **Sao Tome & Principe:** UNICEF; **Saudi Arabia:** Rex Hamaker; **Serbia:** Bukola A. Jejeloye, Aleksandra Kostic, Slobodan Acketa; **Seychelles:** Bernadette Dogley; **Sierra Leone:** UNICEF; **Singapore:** Kamil Gamanski & Izabela Frycz; **Slovakia:** Andrea & Tomas Halasz, Anna & Roman Jurkech; **Slovenia:** Ursa Potocnik; **South Africa:** Sophie & Benjamin Narcyz; **Spain:** Sonia Torres, Felix Slager & Valerie Lamy; **Sri Lanka:** Benjamin Beeckmans; **St. Lucia:** Marcella & Lee Klejnot; **St. Vincent:** Helena Nyhlen; **Sudan:** Violetta Polese; **Sweden:** Nanna Sundkvist; **Switzerland:** Marcia & Massimo Depol, Claire-Agnes Chave; **Tajikistan:** UNICEF; **Tanzania:** Cyrille Falisse & Celia; **Thailand:** Klongboon Family; **Trinidad & Tobago:** Annie Henry; **Tunisia:** Douda Anouar & Jazz; **Turkey:** Benardete Family; **United Arab Emirates:** Regina Maniaci & Craig Delery; **United Kingdom:** Jessica Smith; **Ukraine:** Anna & Hennady; **Uruguay:** Irina Raffo; **United States of America:** James Wasser, Phil Micali, Valentina Cassata; **Uzbekistan:** Igor Kolomiychenko; **Venezuela:** Elena & Raul Serey; **Vietnam:** Benjamin Attar, SOS Children's Village Ben Tre; **Zambia:** Brooke Family.

Our Donors

Bahamas: Brenda McCartney; **Belgium:** Ana Moreno Morales, Aurian Van Ongevalle, Berengere Ronse, Bertrand Bodson, Carine Hellemans, Carolone Aeby, Chantal van Cutsem, Claude Fontaine, Daniel Dawance, Daphne Gevers, Edmond de la Haye, Eliane Teirlinck, Eloise Lagrenee, Emilie Hepner, Emmanuel Jacubowitz, Aeby Lamfalussy Family, Asselberghs-Burgelman Family, Biard-Winders Family, Bruno Van Lierde Family, Caeymaex-Kaeckenbeeck Family, Castaigne-Jassogne Family, Catherine Cos, Claes Vandereeckt Family, Degreef Family, Faelli-Hallin Family, Fontaine-Pont Family, Galere-Goossens Family, Lemaigre-Desmarets Family, Leunen-Brion Family, Liessens Dujardin Family, Obozinski-Lavaud Family, Van Cauwenberghe Family, Van Daele-de Paepe Family, VanWalle-Willemse Family, Verschueren-Lemaigre Family, Wanet Family, Francine Delahaye, Frederic VanParijs, Gerard Pierson, Germain Stordiau, Groep Verbaet, Hans Verheggen, Isabelle Lesser, Jacinte Monsieur, Jean Paul Christope, Jean Thys, Jean-Francois Gosse, Jean-Pierre Beernaerts, Jean-Pierre Herman, Jean-Yves Charlier, Laura Giblin, Laurence Ricart, Laurent Violon, Laurent Wanet, Luc de Brabandere, Lucie Peeters, Marcelo Goldstein, Marie Laure Lasson, Martine Delbeke, Michel Alle, Michel Carlier, Michel Theissen, Michelle Storms, Moira Riley, Nirina Rabemiafara & Desire Magbunduku, Patricia Decuypere, Patrick Asael, Patrick Somerhausen, Patrick Tondreau, Philippe De Backer, Philippe Loncke, Philippe Mathei, Philippe Monheim, Philippe Segers, Pierre Cambier, Robert Cohen, Sabine Schanzer, Sandrine & Bruno Hellemans, Schaub Family; Simone Prebois, Steigrad Family; Sylvie André-Dumont, Thierry Vanwelkenhuyzen, Tom Kimpe, Valerie Nowak, Xavier Vidal, Yvette Haker; **Central African Republic:** Patrick Asael; **Chile:** Andres & Claudia Serey, Patrick Jadoul & Barbara Morana, Francisco Pezo, Soledad & Christian Kaczorowski; **China:** Fabrice Marcotty; **Ethiopia:** Anteneh Meseret; **France:** Cathy Bangala, Claudie Noe-Wilson, Marie Barthe, Marisoa Ramonja, Soary Andrianarisoa, Tovo Radanielson; **Israel:** David Elkaim Family; **Italy:** Francesca Caporali Family, Jasmin Battista, Luca Tognoli, Raphael Caporali; **Lithuania:** Egle Satkute; **Madagascar:** Martine Catry; **Mexico:** Marylou & Jose Israel Capuano, Monica del R Duran; **Netherlands:** Andy Zijlmans, Ayman van Bregt; **Peru:** Carlos Medina; **Serbia:** Goldmund Lukic; **Sweden:** Andreas Johansson; **Switzerland:** Marcia & Massimo dePol; **Trinidad & Tobago:** Phyllis Hoyte; **Turkey:** Albert Benardete Family, Füsun Aydinlik, Guzin Tezel; **United Kingdom:** Alena Shiryaeva, Deborah Lewis, Nadia Kazolides, Paul Knigth, Tom Koukoulis; **United States of America:** Christina Eater, Micali Family, John Bland, Jonathan Walker, Julie Rogers, Kathy Adams, Lilian Petty, Linda Tom, Margaret Richards, Marie Barthe, Marina Massi, Mark Israel, Priscilla Rodrigues, Regine Korn, Stacey Warren, Will Lubart.

Our Local Partners

Armenia: Peace Corps Volunteers; **Belgium:** Radio Judaica; **Benin:** Regard de la Jeunesse; **Bhutan:** V.A.S.T.; **Bolivia:** Junta Vecinos El Alto; **Botswana:** iEarn; **Brazil:** Saude Sem Limites, Mundo Livre; **Burkina Faso:** Association Espoir pour Demain; **Cape Verde:** Associação Crianças Desfavorecidas; **China:** Handicap International; **Congo:** Azur Development; **Cote d'Ivoire:** Club des Amis de la Culture Universelle; **Dominica:** Peace Corps Volunteers; **Finland:** Pääkaupunkiseudun Omaishoitajat ja Läheiset; **Gabon:** BD Boom; **Gambia:** Bajito Onda Africa; **Germany:** Color Value; **Haiti:** Fondation Culture Creation; **Iraq:** Diakonia; **Madagascar:** AGSP Pact; **Maldives:** National Center for Arts; **Moldova:** Step by Step; **Korea, North (DPRK):** Koryo Group; **Laos:** Children Education & Development Center; **Liberia:** Child Art Liberia; **New Zealand:** One People One Planet; **Paraguay:** Fe y Alegria; **Peru:** Fundación Coprodeli; **South Africa:** Lebo Children Center; **St. Kitts & Nevis:** Peace Corps Volunteers; **St. Lucia:** Peace Corps Volunteers; **Togo:** Volontariat Secours et Vie; **Uganda:** Maison des Enfants du Monde; **Venezuela:** Centro de Educación Popular de Santa Rosa de Agua.

Our Global Partners

UNICEF
Fundación América
SOS Children's Villages
Maison des Enfants du Monde
Hughes Hubbard & Reed

Our Board of Directors

Anthony Asael, Benoit Seys, Hans Verheggen, Louis Philippe Loncke, Raphael Guilbert, Regis Verschueren, Sibylle Smets, Stéphanie Rabemiafara

Our Board of Advisers

Egidio Crotti (Chile), Lilliane Petty (USA), Lisa Tucci (Italy), Michael Jacobs (Belgium), Roberto Edwards (Chile), Ruggero Gabbai (Italy), Sharad Sapra (USA)

Our Corporate Sponsors

Acadian	Jainco Tech	Salesforce
Altavia	Kick & Rush	S.F. Investments
Applica	Latham and Watkins	Toledo Telecom
Art Venture	Lowepro	Touring
D'Ieteren	Netway	Weinberg Travel Agency
DreamSakes	PricewaterhouseCoopers	Windiam
Isabel	Promethan	
It's so Good	Publi-Market	

What about you?

If you wish to support our efforts or help fund our activities, visit our Web site: www.artinallofus.org/i-want-to-support-donate.html

Fundación América

And a very special thank you to the whole team at Fundación América in Chile, who helped us during four years, and particularly to Roberto Edwards.

Bárbara Astaburuaga, Marcelo Ayala, Fabián Carrasco, Jeampiere Dinamarca, Teresita Errázuriz, María Isabel Fernández, María Inés Fuenzalida, Marie Caroline Gravereaux, Felipe Hernández, Paty Leiva, Mauricio Miranda, Rogelio Orozco, Pedro Quevedo, Roberto Severino, Rodrigo Yáñez.

Biographies

Anthony Asael

Anthony Asael was born in 1974 in Brussels, prematurely, impatient to discover our beautiful world. He said his first words twenty-four months later, to the great relief of his parents. At the age of five, he went on his first solo travel—on an inflatable boat, willing to cruise the Mediterranean Sea—to which his mother reacted by telling him stories of his grandfather and his passion for photography, hoping to slow down Anthony's precocious interest for exploration. Anthony's curiosity was indeed piqued and at seven years old, he started developing his own photographs in a darkroom. Three years later, he read his first Jules Verne novel, and bought his first world map. He had to wait until he turned seventeen to leave on a new solo adventure in southern and eastern Europe, rucksack on his back, and camera in his hands.

Five years of serious studies then followed at Solvay Business School. A dreamer, he started his professional life as a truck driver. He realized quite fast, however, that he wouldn't make it across the oceans driving his truck. He then agreed to organize the commercial mission of H.M. the Prince Philip of Belgium in India. Having inherited his grandfather's professional camera, he rediscovered his early passion for photography. At age twenty-three, after a fortunate series of less-than-fortunate events, he found himself selling bananas at a market, in a small village of southern Bangladesh. Three years later, he met for the first time Stéphanie Rabemiafara's sparkling and dreamy eyes. The same year, he won the Prince Albert Fund fellowship, and left to go to Chile as the manager of a Belgian company's subsidiary in Latin America. He, of course, didn't forget to pack his camera. He had his first photo exhibition in Bolivia in 2000, followed soon by a second and a third one in Chile and Brazil.

At age twenty-eight, he learned his sixth language, Portuguese, and met again with Stéphanie. They founded Art in All of Us together in 2005. Anthony left his tie and suit in his closet for good, and visited the first school of their journey in Guyana. The following four years, he visited the world schools together with Stéphanie, in order to stimulate children's creativity and curiosity. In 2006, he learned that a photographer's life can be as exciting as a spy's, as he spent his first hours in a Jordanian jail. During 2007, Anthony slept in 131 different beds, and thought to himself that without people's hospitality, this project would have never been achieved. He celebrated his thirty-fourth birthday in North Korea, happy that Art in All of Us was the first foreign artistic project to be granted official entry in North Korean schools. He was later invited by the United Nations in New York to exhibit Art in All of Us photographs and artwork for the twentieth anniversary of the Convention on the Rights of the Child. More than sixty-five exhibitions have already been organized, illustrating both Anthony's and Stéphanie's photographs and creations.

Stéphanie Rabemiafara

Stéphanie Rabemiafara was born in 1979 in Madagascar, curious, with a sweet tooth; she was a dreamer, impatient and talkative. Her interest for development matters started at an early age, and kept on pursuing her during her studies and personal projects. She has worked as a financial auditor in Belgium and Chile, before founding Art in All of Us with her life partner, Anthony Asael.

Her passion for travels also developed at an early age, an inspiration that came from her foreigner school friends, who were passing from one country to another. They had lived in Mauritania, Switzerland, or China, and were leaving to Mozambique, Bolivia, or Malaysia. Stéphanie learned to travel with them, sharing typical dishes they had learned "in other lands." A dreamer, plenty of projects were already mushrooming in her head.

Her passion for photography? She was almost born with it. Her eye for photography, for photogenic landscapes, and her skills at researching and capturing a perfect angle, a moment, a look, or an attitude, came from her grandfather. She invested her first paychecks from student jobs into a professional photographic camera, following without knowing, a family tradition.

She started this tour of children's lands intimidated by their wide-open eyes at the sight of those two strangers, who came for the day to teach and share. She discovered relativity: the relativity of time, friendship, encounters, involvement, and the color of the skin. She let herself become a chameleon, changing skin from country to country. In Guinea, she was white, and her hair was an absolute fascination for the school's girls. In Estonia, a school girl took her hand, and gave it back to her after a careful searching, confessing she was quite brown! She learned she could be a Latino, an Asian, or even someone from Oceania. She learned to eat with her hands, and she discovered that she liked it. She learned to bend like an accordion in a bush-taxi, and to stay in the same position for tens of hours, sharing the space with twenty other fellow travelers, in the heat and in the dust. She learned to laugh when she couldn't understand one word, and then, when she understood everything; she learned to laugh when she agreed and then when she didn't agree as much. But most of all, she learned to understand. Her photographs have traveled around the world in exhibits organized by Art in All of Us.

MAZAR-E SHARIF • 2008

KORCÉ • 2007

ALGIERS • 2008

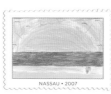
SANT JULIA DE LORIA • 2008

LUANDA • 2007

SAINT JOHN'S • 2007

RESISTENCIA • 2006

YEREVAN • 2007

BRISBANE • 2006

VIENNA • 2008

BAKU • 2007

NASSAU • 2007

MANAMA • 2009

JESSORE • 2006

FARMERS • 2007

MINSK • 2007

HANDZAME • 2008

EL PROGRESO • 2008

KODE • 2006

THIMPHU • 2006

EL ALTO • 2008

SARAJEVO • 2007

GABORONE • 2008

ALDEIA YUYU DËH • 2006

BANDAR SERI BEWAGAN • 2006

DREN • 2007

BOBO DIOULASSO • 2005

BUJUMBURA • 2008

SIEM REAP • 2006

MAROUA • 2006

TORONTO • 2008

PRAIA • 2005

BANGUI • 2006

MANI KOSSAM • 2008

COYHAIQUE • 2005

CHONGQING • 2006

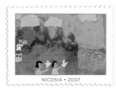
TIERRABOMBA • 2007

MORONI • 2008

KINSHASA • 2007

SAN JOSÉ • 2008

ABIDJAN • 2006

ZAGREB • 2007

LA HAVANA • 2005

NICOSIA • 2007

PRAGUE • 2007

COPENHAGUE • 2008

DJIBOUTI • 2008

GRAND BAY • 2008

SANTO DOMINGO • 2007

IBARRA • 2007

QENA • 2006

SAN SALVADOR • 2008

BATA • 2007

ASMARA • 2008

BRAZZAVILLE • 2007

TALLINN • 2006

ADDIS ABABA • 2008

NADI • 2006

HELSINKI • 2006

AUBERVILLIERS • 2007

LIBREVILLE • 2007

SEREKUNDA • 2005

TBILISSI • 2007

WUPPERTAL • 2008

CAPE COAST • 2006

VARI • 2007

SAINT GEORGE'S • 2007

XEGÜINACABAJ • 2008

BISSAU • 2005

CONAKRY • 2005

BARTICA • 2005

PORT-AU-PRINCE • 2007

CHOLUTECA • 2008

BUDAPEST • 2007

REYKJAVIK • 2008

PHAGI • 2006

JAKARTA • 2006

TEHRAN • 2009

DOHUK • 2007

DUBLIN • 2007

HERZILIAH • 2006

MILANO • 2006

KINGSTON • 2007

TSUSHIMA • 2006

AMMAN • 2006

ALMATY • 2008

KAKAMEGA • 2008

EITA • 2006

SEOUL • 2006

PYONGYANG • 2008

KUWAIT CITY • 2009

TOGUZ-BULAK • 2008

VIENTIANE • 2006

RIGA • 2007

BEYROUTH • 2006

THABA BOSIU • 2008

MONROVIA • 2005

TRIPOLI • 2008

VADUZ • 2008

VILNIUS • 2007

LUXEMBOURG • 2009

SKOPJE • 2007

AMONDRA • 2008

LILONGWE • 2007

AMPANG • 2006

MALE • 2009

NGOA • 2006

MGARR • 2008

DELAP • 2006

NOUAKCHOTT • 2008

TROU AUX BICHES • 2008

SAN MIGUEL • 2008

POHNPEI • 2006

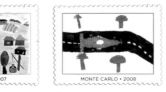
CHISINAU • 2007

MONTE CARLO • 2008

BAGANUUR • 2008

PODGORICA • 2007

BOULAD SGUIR • 2008

ILHA DE MOÇAMBIQUE • 2007

MANDALAY • 2006

WINDHOEK • 2008

NAURU • 2006

KATHMANDU • 2006

HELMOND • 2007

AUCKLAND • 2006

ESTELÍ • 2008

NIAMEY • 2006

JOS • 2006